THE PASS

THE
PASSION AS LITURGY

*A Study in the Origin of the Passion Narratives
in the Four Gospels*

ETIENNE TROCMÉ

SCM PRESS LTD

334 02239 8

First published 1983
by SCM Press Ltd
26–30 Tottenham Road, London N1

Typeset by Gloucester Typesetting Services
and printed in Great Britain by
Richard Clay (The Chaucer Press) Ltd
Bungay, Suffolk

This little book is dedicated to
the University of Glasgow
as a token of gratitude for the conferment of
the degree of Doctor of Divinity

Contents

Preface

This little book dealing with a vast and much-debated topic is based on the Passiontide Lectures delivered from 31 March to 2 April 1980 at Lincoln Theological College. The lectures were somewhat expanded on the occasion of the final redaction, but remained in essence very much the same. This accounts for the cursory nature of a large part of the discussion that follows. All I wanted to achieve was to *suggest* a solution to the problems arising from the plurality of accounts of the sufferings and death of Jesus. For the same reason, notes were kept to a minimum, in spite of the huge literature dealing with the Passion narratives.

Scholars will either pursue the hypothesis further in order to strengthen it or tear it to pieces. In the meantime, may this sketch help some general readers to discover some avenues through the maze of parallel and conflicting accounts of the Passion which we find in the four gospels!

I owe thanks first of all to Canon F. H. A. Richmond, M.A., B.Litt., B.Th., Warden of Lincoln Theological College, whose kind invitation to lecture during the Holy Week of 1980 moved me to commit to writing ideas I had been toying with for a long time. My gratitude also goes to my gracious hosts in Lincoln, among whom a special mention should be made of Mrs Caroline Richmond and of Canon J. S. Nurser, M.A., Ph.D., Chancellor of the College, and Mrs Nurser. Finally, I want to thank my daughter Marie, who took care of the indexes, and my wife, who patiently helped me through the intricacies of the English language.

Etienne Trocmé

INTRODUCTION

The Passion of our Lord Jesus Christ has been for centuries past and still is a favourite object for meditation and prayer, for artistic expression, whether in music or the visual arts, for speculation on the part of theologians, for research by literary critics and historians.

Poets and mystics through the centuries lent their voice to the many humble Christians who contemplated the sufferings, the death and the final triumph of Jesus as recorded in the Passion narratives or as depicted in the works of art based on them. From the hymns of Ephraem Syrus in the fourth century and the *kontakia* of Romanos Melodos in the sixth century to the twentieth-century poems of Paul Claudel and T. S. Eliot, there is a continuous tradition of lyrical expression arising from the devotional reading of the story of the Passion, best summarized perhaps in the well-known refrain coined in the sixteenth century by the French poetess Marguerite de Navarre:

> Penser à la passion
> De Jésus Christ,
> C'est la consolation
> De mon esprit,

or in Richard Crashaw's short poem 'Christ Crucified':

> Thy restless feet now cannot go
>   For us and our eternal good,
> As they were ever wont. What though
>   They swim, alas! in their own flood?

> Thy hands to give Thou canst not lift,
>   Yet will Thy hand still giving be;
> It gives, but O, itself's the gift!
>   It gives tho' bound, tho' bound 'tis free!

I

Similarly, musicians have for nearly two thousand years paid special attention to the moving narrative of the Passion of our Lord and composed all sorts of tunes and pieces meant to be sung or played as those events were commemorated either in private worship or during public liturgies. The 'Passions' of Heinrich Schütz and Johann Sebastian Bach are the best examples of the musical masterpieces thus produced, which to this day mould our understanding of the sufferings, death and resurrection of Jesus Christ.

Needless to say, few scenes from the Bible have been more constantly illustrated by painters and sculptors since the fourth century AD. Most of the episodes of the Passion narratives, from the anointing in Bethany to the appearances of the risen Christ, are known to us through this or that famous painting or sculpture rather more than through a careful reading of the gospels. We imagine the Last Supper as Leonardo da Vinci painted it at Santa Maria delle Grazie in Milan; Judas' Kiss after Cimabue; the *'Ecce Homo'* as Rembrandt saw it; the Crucifixion in the style of Mathias Grünewald's Isenheim altarpiece; the Resurrection as Hans Memling described it; the *'Noli me tangere'* in the manner of Giotto.

Our understanding of the Passion story is also derived to a large extent from the body of doctrine formed through the ages by the efforts of theologians to account for the scandal of the cross and the meaning of the Resurrection. The medieval debates on the atonement, the modern discussions about the redemptive power of the blood of Christ, the contemporary controversies on the Resurrection as an historical or non-historical event are at the back of our minds and make it very difficult for us to read the texts simply as they are.

Historians of early Christianity and biographers of Jesus have been discussing for two centuries a number of problems raised by the Passion narratives: the chronology of events; legal aspects; the execution of Jesus; the topography of the main scenes, etc. Many of the questions they raise are relevant and cannot be simply dismissed.

Finally, literary critics and commentators analyse the various versions of the story of Christ's Passion with such great acumen that every sentence, every clause, every word in it calls to mind a conjecture, a parallel or even a whole learned debate. Scholarship becomes a screen between discriminating readers and the text.

In other words, few texts have ever attracted so much attention on the part of so many people. This is a sobering thought for anybody trying to study the Passion narrative. He stands little chance of breaking new ground and of opening new avenues. As a matter of fact, in our attempt at seeing *The Passion as Liturgy*, we shall see at every corner signs saying 'So and so was here'.

In spite of that, some of the ideas expressed here may strike the readers as new, or odd, or even unlikely, because I shall here and there side with scholars holding minority views and at some points put forward hypotheses which cannot be totally verified and thus remain simply suggestions offered for further thinking and discussion. This may be due to a peculiar state of mind on my part, but there is more to it than just that.

In spite of the efforts made by artists, theologians and scholars of yesterday and today, we do not yet understand early Christianity to the full, nor do we know Jesus of Nazareth so well either. There is still plenty of room for research and interpretation. This applies in particular to the Passion narratives, both as documents on the last days of Jesus and as texts witnessing to some aspects of early Christian life.

Thus the reviving of this or that minority view of yesteryear or the construction of new hypotheses is part of a vast collective effort to reach a full understanding of those texts and of the events they record. Even tentative suggestions and conclusions are in order and may contribute something to our knowledge of the birth of the Christian faith.

No attempt will be made here to reconstruct the historical episodes of the trial and execution of Jesus.[1] My single aim will be to make a comparative study of the Passion narratives found in the canonical gospels, which are undoubtedly the oldest extant accounts of the sufferings and death of Jesus and have much in common. It is generally agreed[2] that those four narratives acquired their present form no later than AD 100, that is much earlier than any other Passion story found in apocryphal gospels like the Gospel according to Peter.[3] This suggests of course that they may have some historical value as sources for a biography of Jesus. But it also suggests that there may be a close connexion between the four texts. Written in the same language in the same century for readers belonging to various groups of the same small religious movement, those narratives tell the same story in roughly the same order. It would be very surprising indeed if there was no literary relationship between them.

Once we have solved that problem, we can go beyond the texts as they are and reconstruct in part the tradition behind them. This tradition of course has a place in the life of early Christian congregations, a *Sitz im Leben*, as the specialist's jargon calls it. If we discover what that 'place in life' is, we shall be very much the wiser about the deep feelings and liturgical customs of our distant forefathers – a fascinating prospect indeed!

But this is no easy task. The four narratives we have in front of us are similar in a number of ways, but different – even widely different – in many others. Before we turn to anything else, we must take a very close look at each of them and compare it with the others.

PART I

THE FOUR PASSION NARRATIVES

I

Mark *14-16* and Mark *1-13*

Since the Gospel according to Mark is considered by a vast majority of scholars as the oldest of our canonical gospels, let us begin with it.

One of the main puzzles of that gospel is its strange ending. The women who have just found the tomb of Jesus open and a young man in a white robe sitting there are informed by this mysterious messenger that the body of their Master is no longer there, because Jesus the Nazarene has risen from the dead (16.4–6). Then they are told by the same angel to go and inform the disciples and notably Peter that Jesus is going before them to Galilee, where they will see him (v. 7). But, as v. 8 puts it: 'They went out and ran away from the tomb; they were shaken and out of their wits. They said nothing to anybody; they were frightened.'

Although many of the manuscripts add after this verse either a long ending (12 verses) or a short one (2 sentences), or even a conflation of the two, the best manuscripts and the scholars among the Fathers (Clement of Alexandria, Origen, Eusebius, Jerome) make it quite clear that the gospel ends with v. 8 and that the other conclusions are later attempts at improving what was felt to be an unbearably crude end for the story of Jesus.[4]

Unbearably crude it is indeed. How could the conclusion of the gospel have been that the good news of the Resurrection of the Lord, so central to Christian faith, had got lost on its way to the people who were to witness to it? The good news announced in Mark 1.1 simply cannot come to its close with a mere mention of the fear which accounts for the failure of the women to carry out the mission entrusted to them by an angel of God! But at the same time, the rationalized endings found in so many manuscripts simply cannot be declared authentic.

Some scholars react to this impossible state of affairs by assuming that the original ending of the Markan gospel got lost by accident or was suppressed at an early date because it was not compatible with what had in the meantime become the orthodox doctrine of the Resurrection. But a suppression caused by theological motives is most unlikely for all sorts of reasons: it would have to be dated very early, no later than the beginning of the second century AD, that is at a time when no orthodoxy had yet prevailed among the Christian churches and when these differed openly on some aspects of the Resurrection of Christ, if we judge from the widely diverging stories found in the last chapters of the other canonical gospels; it is hard to imagine a clumsier use of the censor's scissors, when it would have been so easy to make the cut at the end of v. 7 or to hide it by adding one or two explanatory sentences at the end of v. 8, just as was done much later (fourth or fifth century AD?) when the shorter ending was written; etc. . . . We need not therefore pay any attention to that arbitrary conjecture.[5]

As for the hypothesis of an accidental loss of part of the original text, it cannot be based on some conjecture about an unexpected event that would have brought the writing of the book to a sudden end. Even if the evangelist had died or been arrested unexpectedly, his book did not get lost. The people who copied and distributed it would no doubt have added a brief conclusion to the unfinished work, had such a situation arisen. We have no trace of such an addition, since the endings we find in the manuscripts are much later. The only possible cause for an accidental loss of the original ending would be a situation in which the writer's own manuscript was somehow damaged after the evangelist had lost sight of it and before copies had been made of it. But this hypothesis is so complicated and unlikely that we have to discard it too.[6]

This being the case, we are left with the problem of a gospel ending in an impossible way.[7] To make matters even more complicated, there are the verses in the last chapters of the Markan gospel which would be very satisfactory conclusions for the whole book. For instance, the centurion's christological confession in 15.39 would be a very effective ending for a gospel which could then be read as a gradual disclosure of Jesus' divine sonship, if it could be shown that the burial (15.42–46) and the empty tomb (16.1–8) are an appendix introduced by two lists of women witnesses intended as a link between the crucifixion and the discovery of the empty tomb (15.40f.

and 15.47). What makes that conjecture unlikely is the fact that it puts the emphasis on messianic titles to a degree which is not compatible with Mark's restraint in using them.[8]

An even better example of a hidden conclusion for the whole Markan gospel is the call to wakefulness in 13.33–37, since it ends in v. 37 with this generalizing remark: 'And what I say to you, I say to everyone: stay awake!' Those words make it clear that every reader of the gospel is called upon to apply to himself all the exhortations addressed in 13.3–36 to Peter, James, John and Andrew. But is that all? The story of Jesus, as it is told in chs. 1–12, is not a biography beginning with the birth and childhood of the hero in the style of Matthew and Luke; it is a vigorous call to action and to self-sacrifice in the steps of the Master; this call aimed at the hearers of Jesus' preaching is doubtless meant all along for the readers of the gospel, although that remains implicit; 13.37 states openly what had so far been left unsaid: any reader of the book has to consider Jesus' exhortations as addressed to himself.

As a confirmation of this interpretation of 13.37, let us remind ourselves that the Markan gospel is a succession of groups of anecdotes in which Jesus plays the leading part, but is constantly surrounded by the disciples, who have to draw for their own life and mission the lessons of what they see and hear. Those lessons include the acceptance of suffering and even death, just as Jesus himself accepted them according to 8.31, 9.31 and 10.32–34, and the certainty of final victory, as exemplified in Jesus' triumph in Jerusalem (chs. 11 and 12) and as promised in the apocalyptic discourse in ch. 13. Since that discourse is thus closely linked with the chapters preceding it, it comes as no surprise that its conclusion in vv. 33–37 applies to the whole book and offers the key for reading it properly.

In other words, what follows that conclusion – i.e. the Passion narrative in chs. 14–16 – might be seen as a kind of *appendix* to the main body of the gospel. As a matter of fact, the general perspective in the story of the Passion differs in a number of ways from that in chs. 1–13. The Passion narrative is much more biographical in style than the rest of the gospel: Jesus goes his own way to the cross in ever-growing isolation, as if to show that his sufferings and his death, although they were achieved for us, cannot be shared by his disciples, who are no longer called upon to follow in the Master's steps; instead of being asked to deny themselves, take up their cross and walk behind Jesus, they are invited to share symbolically in his death by partaking of the Eucharist. That feature of the Passion narrative is enough to show how different it is from chs. 1–13. But the difference might be due to there being different traditional backgrounds behind the two sections combined into one by the evangelist.

In order to support this minimizing thesis, much has been made of the lack of any difference in vocabulary and style between chs. 1–13 and chs. 14–16. We shall come back to this point soon.[9] Suffice it to say for the time being that the Gospel of Mark, from beginning to end, makes no claim whatever to literary style, as Matthew and Luke both do, each in its own way, nor does it show any sign of personal style, as would be the case with the Fourth Gospel. It is written the way people spoke, which simply means that the traditions it made use of and the evangelist himself had had no contact with educated circles. The argument derived from its style is therefore very weak.

It has been claimed also that many of the features of Mark 1–13 pointed towards the Passion narrative,[10] so that these chapters must be seen as a long introduction to the story of the sufferings, death and resurrection of Jesus, which is the real core of the gospel.[11] For instance, the allusion to 'the days when the bridegroom is taken away from them' (2.20) is seen as a prophecy of the Passion and thus, in literary terms, as an announcement that the story of those tragic 'days' will follow further in the same book. Or again, it is said that the conspiracy of the Pharisees and the Herodians against the life of Jesus (3.6) prepares the way for that of the 'high priests and scribes' at the beginning of ch. 14 (vv. 1f. and 10f.). Again, if Judas Iscariot is introduced as 'the man who betrayed him' (3.19), is it not – some scholars ask – to warn the reader that he will find some betrayal scenes at a later stage in the gospel (14.10f., 43–45)?

The answer to all the remarks made to that effect is simply that Mark 1–13 is full of allusions and prophecies of the *fact* of Jesus' sufferings, death and resurrection, but none of those passages points to a *narrative* of these events which would be part of the same book. No story is needed for the readers to know what the allusions and prophecies in question are about, since the Passion of our Lord was at the heart of Christian preaching. No story is announced by those allusions and prophecies, since these often point also to the Resurrection of Christ, which is nowhere narrated in the gospel, but only announced to the women at the tomb (16.6). Thus, if the Markan Passion narrative is found to be an appendix, mentions of the Passion elsewhere in the gospel can stand on their own feet; they are explicit enough (see 8.31; 9.31; 10.32–34) to make it quite clear what it means to follow in the steps of Jesus, which is the evangelist's main aim.

In order to reach a final decision about the relationship between chs. 14–16 and the main body of the Gospel of Mark, the question must be raised whether there are any contradictions between them. As a matter of fact, there are. To name but a few, let us come back to a point which we mentioned earlier: the attitudes of the two sections towards christological titles. In chs. 1–13, the use of titles like Son of man, Son of God and Christ is not frequent (10, 5 and 5 times) and is discouraged by Jesus himself (see 3.11f.; 5.7f.; 8.29f.; 9.9–13). In the Passion narrative, which is less than one fourth of chs. 1–13 in length, the same titles are used more often (4, 2 and 2 times) and raise no objection on the part of Jesus (see 14.61f.; 15.39), who accepts being anointed by the woman (14.3–9) and being called King of the Jews by Pilate (15.2; see 15.26). There is a clear difference here.

Another difference concerns Jesus' attitude towards the temple. In 13.2, the Master predicts the ruin of this splendid monument – a prophecy which we read also in the parallels of Matt. 24.2 and Luke 21.5f. But in Mark 14.57–59, Jesus is accused *falsely* of having said that he would destroy the temple and then rebuild it. Matthew felt that there was an inescapable contradiction between those two texts, so much so that he toned down the whole episode of the testimonies against Jesus during the meeting of the Sanhedrin (26.59–61): instead of a number of witnesses, he mentions only two, who are indeed not said to have been truthful, but who at least agree between them, which was not the case with Mark's false witnesses, and who are not branded as liars, except in an indirect way; in addition, the accusation they level at Jesus is only that he claimed he *had the power* to destroy the temple and to rebuild it. Luke simply does away with the whole episode. The contradiction seen by Matthew between Mark 13.2 and Mark 14.57–59 remains to this day and makes it very difficult to admit that the same writer should have put those two passages side by side in his book.

Another contradiction between Mark 1–13 and Mark 14–16 which cannot be explained away, however hard some scholars try, concerns the time that elapsed between the death and the Resurrection of Christ. Mark 15.42 and 16.2 state very clearly that Jesus died on the cross on a Friday evening and that by early morning the following Sunday he *had risen* from the dead and left his tomb. The time interval between the two events was thus at most forty hours, according to the Markan Passion narrative. But in Mark 8.31, 9.31 and 10.33f., it is announced that the Son of man will be killed and then rise again *after three days*. My contention is that the phrase 'after three days' cannot mean 'from a Friday evening to the small hours of the following Sunday morning'. Matthew and Luke were aware of that difficulty, since they both wrote 'on the third day' in the parallels to the three Markan prophecies of the Passion (Matt. 16.21; 17.23; 20.19; Luke 9.22; 18.33). That correction removes the incompatibility of the prophecies of the Passion with the Passion narratives in the synoptic gospels, since the Septuagint (see Hos. 6.2) equates 'on the third day' with 'after two days', just as the Hebrew Bible did. Both these phrases can be applied to the time interval from a Friday evening to the following Sunday morning. It might be objected that Matt. 27.63f. uses the phrases 'after three days' and 'on the third day' in close succession to describe the same period of time. But it is not so: 'after three days' applies to the length of the interval Jesus was said to have announced would elapse between his death and his Resurrection (v. 63); 'until the third day' indicates the time during which it was necessary to keep watch over Jesus' tomb in order to prove that prophecy false, that is, from the Saturday to the Monday following the death (v. 64).

Mark 13.37 is an excellent ending for the Gospel of Mark, since no part of chs. 1–13 points to the presence of a Passion narrative in the same book and some significant divergences are visible between chs. 14–16 and the rest of the gospel. It is therefore a likely conclusion that the Markan Passion narrative is only an appendix added on to the Gospel of Mark.[12] It would thus be foolish to call that gospel 'a Passion narrative with an extended introduction', as Martin Kähler put it nearly a hundred years ago,[13] or to claim with Rudolf Bultmann that in the Gospel of Mark 'the centre of gravity has to be the end of the story, the Passion and Resurrection'.[14] Such phrases only obscure the real facts. The evidence suggests that the Gospel of Mark originally had no room for a Passion narrative. It can even be claimed that chs. 14–16 were appended to that book only after it had existed for some time.[15] They are therefore likely to have had their own history before they were attached to the gospel. To this pre-history we now turn.

2

Mark 14-16 as a pre-Markan unit

The founding fathers of form criticism, writing around 1920, expressed the view that the tradition units brought together by the authors of the synoptic gospels were mostly very short. This, they claimed, became visible as soon as one realized how weak were the links which connected in those three books the brief anecdotes and pithy sayings that form the main part of their contents: vague topographical and chronological notes, plain juxtaposition based on small verbal or logical similarities, generalizing summaries meant to hide the fragmentary nature of the sources used, etc.[16] The only exceptions to that rule were, it was said, the collections of sayings or of anecdotes which had begun to appear in tradition, but had not erased the borderlines between the basic units they were made of, and, secondly, the Passion narratives. These were seen as continuous stories, in which the various episodes were solidly linked with one another. Events followed one another in tight succession. Logically, historically, chronologically, topographically, the sequence of scenes had none of the artificiality and weaknesses so visible in the rest of the synoptic gospels. In other words, those Passion narratives were fairly large literary units long before they were inserted into the gospels.[17]

No one quarrelled with those conclusions for half a century. But the growth of redaction criticism brought with it a tendency to stress more and more the contribution made by the evangelists in writing the gospels. When applied to the study of the Passion narratives, this new approach led some scholars, mostly in Germany and in the United States, to deny the existence of a pre-Markan story of the sufferings and death of Jesus. To name but a few, E. Linnemann and D. Dormeyer in Europe, P. J. Achtemeier, J. R. Donahue and

W. Kelber in North America argue in roughly the same way[18] that the stylistic and theological similarities between Mark 1–13 and Mark 14–16 are so far-reaching and the literary structure of both sections so identical that the redactional work done by the evangelist must have been the same throughout the whole gospel. This writer brought together and combined the same kind of small units of tradition in the Passion narrative as in the rest of his book. He is thus entirely responsible for the order of events and for the interpretation of the sufferings and death of Jesus which is implied in the succession of steps made by the Master on his way to the cross. Let us look at some of the reasons given to support that theory.

There is, those scholars say, a striking similarity between Mark 1–13 and Mark 14–16 as to their style. That is due, it is claimed, to the fact that the evangelist rewrote in his own manner all the traditions he made use of. The trouble is that a clear definition of what Markan usage is was never convincingly given by anyone.[19] Even E. J. Pryke, in his recent monograph on *Redactional Style in the Markan Gospel*, has to admit that 'any neat and tidy solution to the problem of redaction and linguistics in Mark must be ruled out of court'.[20] Quite a few of the Markan characteristics which recede greatly in Matthew and Luke, like the historic present or the use of πάλιν, come in the first place from the traditions used and were borrowed by the evangelist, not coined by him as part of his redactional style. Their rejection by the other two synoptic writers shows that they were felt to be familiar or unliterary, a fact that did not bother Mark, who sees no reason not to write in the loose and lively fashion in which people spoke in everyday life and in oral tradition. This being the attitude of the earliest evangelist as to style, can there be anything like 'Markan usage' which would differ from the style of folk tradition? Is the unity of style from Mark 1 to Mark 16 proof of anything apart from the fact that no effort was made by the writer (or writers?) to give an uplift to the unliterary form of tradition?

In spite of that, E. J. Pryke tries to show that several features which are common in Markan usage and recede in Matthew and Luke might belong to the style of the evangelist and not to that of tradition. He lists fourteen of those characteristics, but for eight of them he has to admit that they existed already in the traditions collected by Mark, who simply widened their use because they were congenial to his own loose way of speaking and writing.[21] Let us have a look at the remaining six.

The first one is the frequent use of parenthetical clauses. If one leaves aside two clumsy scripture quotations (1.1–4 and 7.6–8) and eight translations (3.17; 5.9; 5.41; 7.11f.; 7.34; 12.42; 15.16; 15.34), some of which may well be later additions, we are left with nineteen parenthetical clauses that need no other classification than 'loose sentence construction'. In other words, Mark paid no more attention to sentence construction than tradition had before him and, in spite of Pryke's efforts, there is in most cases no saying who is responsible for the looseness of the sentence. The evangelist makes no attempt at correcting what is loosely said in tradition.[22]

The genitive absolute is used twenty-nine times in Mark. As it is often placed at the beginning of pericopae and usually conveys some topographical or chronological information, it was doubtless a device used by the evangelist to link isolated anecdotes and weave them into a continuous narrative. But some genitive absolutes existed already in tradition, as in 6.21, 22, 35, 47, which cannot be attributed to the evangelist. Neither can we with a sweep of the hand claim for redaction all the occurrences in the first or second verse of a pericope.[23] All we can say, then, is that this very common feature of *koinē* Greek was just as common in the language of early Christians, when they had Greek as their mother tongue, and is in no way a Markan characteristic. The occurrences found in the Markan Passion narrative (14.3, 17, 18, 22, 43, 66; 15.42) thus give us no evidence of a redaction by the evangelist.

The five or six participles used as main verbs may come from the evangelist, but are too few and far between to be significant.[24] Add to this the fact that none of them is found in the Passion narrative.

The ten occurrences of $\pi o \lambda \lambda \acute{a}$ accusative have no significance whatever, considering the widespread use of this word in *koinē* Greek.[25]

The frequent use (41 times) of $\lambda \acute{e} \gamma \omega$ $\acute{o} \tau \iota$ often followed by direct speech is rather colourless, apart from the occurrences beginning with the emphatic $\dot{a} \mu \acute{\eta} \nu$ (3.28; 9.1, 13, 41; 11.23; 12.43; 13.30; 14.18), which there is no reason whatsoever to consider as redactional. Even if a clear majority of the 33 other occurrences were redactional, the use of those two common words and the preference given to direct speech could not be the signs of a personal style. They are just aspects of an artless, plain way of speaking common to tradition and to the evangelist.[26]

Finally, the 26 occurrences of $\check{a} \rho \chi o \mu a \iota$ +infinitive in Mark are doubtless a characteristic of Markan style as opposed to that of Matthew and Luke. But the evangelist certainly found that phrase in his traditional material, where it may have reflected a Semitic idiom. This is quite evident for the seven occurrences in the Passion narrative (14.19, 33, 65, 69, 71; 15.8, 18), but also at several points in chs. 1–13 (1.45; 2.23; 6.2; etc.). Mark found the phrase congenial and put it to use in a fair number of redactional passages. Later, Matthew and Luke thought it was pleonastic and did away with it in most places.[27]

Thus, no redactional style exists in Mark. The unity in style from ch. 1 to ch. 16 only proves that no writer attempted here what Matthew and Luke did later when they gave a literary varnish to their books. It provides no evidence that the Passion narrative was put together and rewritten by the evangelist. It does not even suggest that chs. 14–16 were part of the same book as chs. 1–13, but simply that the traditions behind Mark all come from roughly the same circles.

If no conclusion can be drawn from the style of Mark 14–16, what is the strength of the other approach suggested by the scholars who deny the existence of a pre-Markan Passion narrative: the analysis of the literary structure of Mark's story of the sufferings and death of Jesus? It is claimed that the pericopae are very similar in size and inner structure to those in Mark 1–13 and that the links between them and the overall structure of the narrative are identical to what is found in the main body of the gospel.

It must be granted that some of the pericopae in ch. 14 are self-contained anecdotes which show a clear beginning and a satisfactory end, as well as their own lesson, and can be read for themselves with no reference to their context. The anointing at Bethany (14.3–9), the last meal (14.17–25) and the prayer at Gethsemane (14.32–42) are stories of that kind and may perhaps have led a separate existence at an early stage. Although we cannot be sure of that, other New Testament texts somewhat reinforce that conjecture: Luke 7.36–50 suggests that the story of the anointing was used as a separate unit in preaching; I Cor. 11.23–26 may mean that the story of the last meal was quoted as a separate unit in discussions about community meals in some congregations; the use of ποτήριον as a symbolic name for the Passion in Mark 10.38f. and Matt. 20.22f. indicates perhaps that the Gethsemane prayer was known and referred to in some catechism.

But from the scene of the arrest of Jesus (14.43–52) to the story of the empty tomb (16.1–8), each pericope is closely linked with the others nearest to it. Instead of self-contained units artificially connected together by the evangelist in order to provide illustrations for the main theme of each section of the gospel,[28] we find here a succession of narratives leading to one another and depending on the neighbouring pericopae for their meaning. The arrest scene cannot be understood without referring to the betrayal (14.10f.), the prophecy of the betrayal (14.18–21) and the prayer at Gethsemane (14.32–42), as well as to the trial before the Sanhedrin (14.53–65). Climactic though it is, the scene of the crucifixion (15.22–39) is not self-contained. Its meaning would be difficult to discover if it did not follow the two trials (14.53–65 and 15.2–15) and precede the espisodes of the burial (15.42–47) and of the discovery of the empty tomb (16.1–8). In short, we are confronted with a continuous narrative which has no equivalent in chs. 1–13 either in their final form (the day in Capernaum, 1.21–38, is far shorter and based on two self-contained units from tradition) or in the underlying tradition, where the pre-Markan collections of anecdotes that may have existed (for instance a collection of controversies, as in 2.1–3.6 or in 11.27–12.37) were made up of self-contained units. Thus the literary structure of Mark 14–16 is notably different from that of chs. 1–13.

If one adds that it would be difficult to imagine a separate *Sitz im Leben* for episodes of the Passion taken in isolation, such as the arrest, the trial before Pilate or the empty tomb, it becomes evident that the tradition lying behind the Markan Passion narrative must have been very different from the short self-contained units one still perceives behind chs. 1–13.

The scholars who reject the hypothesis of a pre-Markan Passion narrative also claim that there is a complete theological identity between Mark 1–13 and Mark 14–16. This is not the case. I said earlier that there was a noticeable difference between those two sections as to the use of christological titles.[29] Here lies a far-reaching divergence, which should not be underestimated. The theology of chs. 1–13 is mostly implicit. When it comes to expression, it is mostly christological, but in its own way. Speculative christology is firmly opposed and the evangelist insists that amazed and fearless discipleship is the only possible reaction to the presence of Christ among men. Even key passages like the confession of Peter at Caesarea Philippi (8.27–29) and the definition of Christ's death as 'a ransom for the multitude' (10.45) are placed by Mark in contexts where the call to self-sacrifice as the disciples' lot is unmitigated and central (see 8.30–9.1 and 10.35–44).

On the contrary, chs. 14–16 emphasize very firmly that no disciple is called to share in his Master's sufferings and death: the scenes in Gethsemane are told largely from that angle (see in particular 14.32–34, 37f., 40–42, 47, 50–52) and Peter's denial is seen as the fulfilment of scripture and of a prophecy uttered by Jesus (14.27–31, 54, 66–72) more than as cowardly behaviour; the disciples only share symbolically in Christ's Passion by eating the bread and wine of the Lord's Supper (14.22–25). Besides, Mark 14.24 attributes some kind of sacrificial meaning to the death of Jesus by using the phrase 'my blood of the covenant spilled for the multitude', which has no equivalent in chs. 1–13, where the Passion is only seen as an example to imitate (see 8.31–9.1) and as the payment of 'a ransom for the multitude' (10.45), that is, as a legal-political act.[30]

It is therefore not possible to maintain that chs. 14–16 were the work of the same redactor as Mark 1–13 and received from him the same theological contents as we find in the latter.

My temporary conclusion is that all the evidence favours the majority view that Mark 14–16 is based on a pre-Markan Passion narrative. The exact size and limits, the *Sitz im Leben* and the pre-history of that lengthy tradition unit may be left aside for the time being. I shall come back to those problems later,[31] in order to achieve as clear a picture as possible of that document.

This Passion narrative may of course have been somewhat edited when it became part of the canonical Gospel of Mark. But since it was appended to chs. 1–13 at a later date and in a precarious fashion, this editing was not the work of the evangelist himself and remained slight. No real theological and literary fusion took place.[32] As a result of this, Mark 14–16 resembles very closely the traditional story in its last state before it was incorporated to the gospel.

3

The Passion narrative in Matthew

The Passion narrative which we read in chs. 26–28 of the Gospel according to Matthew is very similar to its Markan counterpart, which we discussed in chapters 1 and 2. Although Matthew, here as in the rest of his book, does quite a bit of editing on the Markan text, in order to do away with over-familiar phrases, with mistakes of grammar or taste, with useless details, etc., his gospel retains nearly all of what Mark had written. Only occasionally does this editing lead to additions of some length in the Passion narrative, whereas such additions are frequent in Matt. 1–25. Let us look at the facts before we try to interpret them.[33]

Matthew 26.1–5 is doubtless based on Mark 14.1f., since vv. 4 and 5 reproduce with minor stylistic changes vv. 1b and 2 of Mark. Verses 1–3 insert the chronological note of Mark 14.1a in a prophecy of Jesus' death made by himself (v. 2), preceded in v. 1 by the redactional transition found at the end of every discourse in Matthew (with two variations about the last three words): καὶ ἐγένετο ὅτε ἐτέλεσεν ὁ Ἰησοῦς τοὺς λόγους τούτους . . . (Matt. 7.28; 11.1; 13.53; 19.1; 26.1), and followed in v. 3 by a brief characterization of the meeting of Jewish leaders implied in the words 'the high priests and the scribes' of Mark 14.1b. This last addition is also editorial, including the name of the high priest Caiaphas, which is never mentioned in Mark, but may have been known to Matthew from the brief midrashic notes on the Passion he used at places to complement the Markan narrative. This introductory pericope, Matt. 26.1–5, gives us an idea of the relationship between the Matthaean Passion narrative and its Markan counterpart: Mark is the source, apart from minor features derived from midrashic notes on the Markan story; the contribution made by the evangelist reinforces the connexion with the rest of the gospel and improves the style and structure of the narrative.

The anointing at Bethany follows (26.6–13), just as in Mark. The only differences are due to corrections made by Matthew to improve the grammar and the style of his source, which was clumsy and long-winded at many places.

The betrayal by Judas (26.14–16) then comes, as in Mark. It is again a close parallel of the Markan story, with much stylistic improvement. A new feature appears: the amount of money given to Judas by the 'high priests', which remained vague in Mark 14.11, is stated in Matthew as being 'thirty pieces of silver'. The origin of this assertion is found in the little *midrash* telling the story of the suicide of the traitor (Matt. 27.3–10), with its quotation from scripture alluding to thirty pieces of silver. Once again, a *midrash* on the Passion story appears as an additional source of the Matthaean Passion narrative beside the Markan narrative.

The story of the Last Supper (26.17–29) differs very little from its Markan parallel, apart from a fair number of stylistic improvements (the somewhat lengthy story of the preparation for the Passover, Mark 14.12–17, is reduced to about three-fifths of its original size; the words of Jesus are slightly edited for clarity's sake) and from the addition of a short dialogue between Judas and Jesus (v. 25), which is doubtless editorial.

As in Mark again, the Gethsemane scenes are then narrated (26.30–56), in the same order as in the Markan parallel and with only minor differences of style, apart from two editorial changes of some consequence: the addition in vv. 52–54 of a pacifist saying of Jesus to the disciple who had struck the servant of the high priest with his sword; the suppression of the concluding episode found in Mark 14.51f., owing no doubt to the irrelevance of the anecdote of the narrow escape of the naked young man in the eyes of Matthew. The Markan narrative (14.26–52) is the only source here.

The trial of Jesus before the Sanhedrin follows (26.57–68), just as in Mark. It is a close parallel of the Markan story, with some editorial changes at various points: the high priest is named (v. 57; see above at v. 3); in vv. 59 to 63a, the quest for testimonies against Jesus is somewhat shortened and cleverly edited in order to avoid the contradiction with the beginning of the synoptic apocalypse which is so striking in the appendix to Mark (see above, p. 11); in vv. 63c and 65b, the words of the high priest are expanded by the

evangelist in order to make it quite clear that the Sanhedrin condemned Jesus to death for blasphemy; in v. 64a the Master's reply
to the high priest is also edited so that Jesus' blasphemy consists,
not in asserting his messiahship (as in Mark), but in his implied
claim to be the Son of man; finally, vv. 67f. are edited in such a
way that all the blows given to Jesus come from the Sanhedrites,
whereas Mark 14.65 attributed part of them to the servants. Once
again, Mark is the only source here.

Peter's denial is then narrated (26.69–75), as in Mark. Although
the two stories are not identical, there is no doubt that the Markan
narrative is the only source of the Matthaean one. The differences
all aim at shortening uselessly long sentences of Mark (see vv. 69,
70b, 71, 74) or at clarifying confused ones (see vv. 72, 73b, 75), if
we leave aside a few purely verbal changes. The dramatic progression attached to the triple denial is not only preserved, but even
underlined in Matthew thanks to the growing firmness of Peter's
declarations, which does not come out so clearly in the Markan
narrative: ἠρνήσατο (v. 70) ... ἠρνήσατο μετὰ ὅρκου (v. 72) ...
ἤρξατο καταθεματίζειν καὶ ὀμνύειν ὅτι οὐκ οἶδα ... (v. 74). This
progression is totally lacking in the Lukan story, where the drama-
tization lies mostly in the look thrown by Jesus at his disciple after
the third denial (Luke 22.61a), a feature unknown to the other
canonical gospels.

This story is followed, in Matthew as in Mark, by a short note on
the handing over of Jesus to Pilate (27.1f.). The rather clumsy
sentence of Mark 15.1 is vastly improved by the Matthaean emendations, which produce a reasonably clear picture of the early morning
meeting of the Sanhedrin so poorly described in the Markan
parallel. Matthew has no other source and Luke and John differ
widely from the first two gospels at this point.

Matthew 27.3–10 is the first of the two pericopae inserted by the
author of the first gospel into the fabric of the Markan Passion
narrative, leaving aside the additions made within pericopae. As I
said earlier about 26.14–16, this story of the death of Judas is a sort
of *midrash* grafted in Matthaean circles on the betrayal episode of
the Passion narrative in its Markan form.[34] The narrative of Acts
1.16–20 is not a close parallel, although its theme is similar.

With the lengthy episode of the trial before Pilate (27.11–26), the
parallelism with the Markan Passion narrative is resumed. The order
of events is exactly the same and there are relatively few verbal

emendations, owing no doubt to the fairly clear redaction of the Markan parallel. The cuts are very limited, for the same reason. Conversely, there is an unusually large number of additions, some of them meant as clarifications of the narrative (vv. 11a, 12b, 21b), others offering fresh information: the dream of Pilate's wife (v. 19) and Pilate's washing of hands (vv. 24f.), both midrashic in origin.

Matthew 27.27–32 tells, just as the Markan parallel (Mark 15. 16–21), of the mocking of Jesus by the soldiers and of his way to Golgotha. Apart from some slight changes in words, the Matthaean redaction only adds that the crown of thorns was put on the head of our Lord and the reed in his right hand (v. 29b) and does away with some useless details concerning Simon of Cyrene. This is purely editorial.

The crucifixion narrative (27.33–54) follows closely the Markan parallel (15.22–39) and rearranges it only from place to place. There is just one significant cut: the sentence indicating the time of the crucifixion (Mark 15.25). But there are several additions worth mentioning: vv. 34 (part), 37 (part), 40c, 43, 51b–53, 54 (part). The longest of these (vv. 51b–53) comes from some *midrash* on the Passion; vv. 34 and 43 contain scriptural allusions which are likely to be a contribution of the evangelist;[35] the other three are editorial. Thus, the only source is the Markan narrative, apart from the *midrash* used to describe the strange events caused by the death of Jesus.

The list of women witnessing the crucifixion from afar (27.55f.) follows the centurion's confession of faith, as in Mark. It has been rewritten by Matthew, who is responsible for all the changes, even about the names given to those women and to their relatives.

Next we have the story of Jesus' burial (Matt. 27.57–61), as in the Markan narrative. It is a somewhat shortened version of it. The only addition worthy of a mention is the description of the tomb as being new and belonging to Joseph of Arimathaea (v. 60a) – editorial remarks no doubt.

Then comes the story of the guard at the tomb (Matt. 27.62–66), an addition that has no counterpart in Mark, nor anywhere in the canonical gospels. It is closely connected with 28.11–15 and has a strong apologetic flavour. It is certainly based on a tradition which is best described as a *midrash* on the story of the empty tomb.

The parallelism with Mark is resumed with that narrative (28. 1–8), but Matthew must have found the Markan version particularly unsatisfactory, because he rewrote it from beginning to end without altering its outline. Verse 1 is a greatly shortened form of Mark 16.1–4; vv. 2–4 alter and develop considerably Mark 16.5 in order to make it quite clear who the divine messenger was and to solve the problem raised by the presence of some guards near the tomb; vv. 5–8 run parallel to Mark 16.6–8, but considerably edit this strange passage: the women are to announce Jesus' resurrection (v. 7b) and not simply that the Master will meet his disciples in Galilee; they feel afraid, but also glad at the news (v. 8a); they actually deliver the message (v. 8b). All those changes are editorial.

As is well known, various post-Resurrection episodes then follow in Matt. 28.9–20. They have no counterpart in Mark, nor in Luke and John, although the latter two also have their own post-Resurrection scenes. The Matthaean narratives bear the mark of the evangelist's editorial activity, particularly in vv. 16–20, which are the solemn epilogue of the gospel. But the appearance of Jesus to the women (vv. 9f.) and, as I said earlier, the false rumour spread among the Jews (vv. 11–15) both seem based on a *midrash* about the empty tomb.

As appears from this comparative review of the Passion narratives of Matthew and Mark, Matthew had at his disposal a copy of the Gospel of Mark including the appendix. This was his only source for chs. 26–28 apart from a few midrashic traditions (26.3, 15b; 27.3–10, 19, 24f., 51b–53, 62–66; 28.9f., 11–15) which have no close parallel in the other canonical gospels and therefore are most likely to have developed in the Matthaean circles, whatever and wherever these may have been.[36] The editorial activity of the evangelist was considerable, in spite of the fact that he did not have to cope in the Passion narrative with the problems he faced in other parts of the gospel, where he had to combine sources into a coherent whole and to bring order when he felt Mark was confused. He provided the Passion narrative with an editorial introduction which linked it effectively with the rest of the gospel (26.1) and an editorial conclusion which serves also as the conclusion of the whole gospel (28.16–20). He inserted the additional material he had chosen to use, whether borrowed from a *midrash* or purely editorial, at the right places in the narrative. He rewrote all that had been left unclear or expressed in a style too loose or too familiar in his main source.

This being said, the Matthaean Passion narrative retains so much of the structure and contents of its Markan counterpart that there can be no doubt as to their close relationship. The order of events is identical throughout, the chronology and topography of both narratives are exactly the same, most of the episodes are told in closely similar ways – as in the case of Peter's denial (cf. Matt. 26.69–75 and Mark 14.66–72). As we shall see later, the parallelism that exists here is a good deal closer than any other relationship that could be detected between Passion narratives, even though there are many similarities between all of them.

Theoretically, this state of affairs could also be interpreted as a sign of the priority of the Matthaean narrative over the Markan one, particularly if we are prepared to consider the latter as an appendix to the original Gospel of Mark, since it can then be dated fairly late. But in fact, various reasons compel us to reject that conjecture: why should Matthew's smooth ending have vanished in Mark and not have been replaced at all? how could one account for the loss of stories like the suicide of Judas and the appearance of the risen Christ to the women? Could we understand the elimination of a meaningful saying of Jesus like Matt. 26.52–54? A third hypothesis would be to explain the close relationship between the Matthaean and the Markan Passion narratives by the use of a common source. This is not likely, if Matthew is based largely on Mark 1–13; the parallelism between Matt. 26–28 and Mark 14–16 being similar in every way to that existing between the rest of those two gospels, it is best to consider the Markan Passion narrative as the direct source of the last three chapters in Matthew.

Thus the Matthaean Passion narrative does not help us much in our effort to go back as far as possible into the early literary history of the tradition concerning the Passion of our Lord. It gives us interesting information about early midrashic embroideries made on the fringes of a coherent written story of the sufferings and death of Jesus in some Christian circles in the 80s. In other words, it offers us some limited insights into the early forms of apocryphal Passion narratives. It also gives us an idea of the way people felt in those circles about some aspects of the Passion: the fulfilment of God's will as expressed in scripture (26.54; 27.9f.); Jewish guilt in the death of Jesus (27.24f.); Jesus' rejection of violence, a paradigm for the disciples (26.52f.); the cosmic meaning of the death of our Lord (27.51–53); the boundless authority of the risen Christ and

world mission as consequences of the Resurrection (28.16–20).
Important though all that is, we are sent back to the Markan
Passion narrative if we want to tackle the problem of the birth and
growth of the story of the sufferings and death of Jesus. Will the
situation be the same with the Lukan and the Johannine narratives?

4

The Passion narrative in Luke

It becomes clear at first glance that the relationship between the Lukan Passion narrative and its counterparts in Mark and Matthew is not as intimate as the one which we discovered between the latter two.

The Lukan Passion narrative is about the same length as that of Matthew: 180 verses to Matthew's 161 verses, as against 127 in Mark. But it differs from it, as well as from Mark's story, in a number of ways.

The most noticeable difference is that none of the Matthaean additions to the Markan text is found in Luke. On the contrary, Luke's narrative contains features that are not compatible with those additions and do not even try and correct them. For instance, Acts 1.16–20 gives a version of Judas' death which cannot be reconciled with Matthew's story of his suicide (Matt. 27.3–10); the christophany granted to the women according to Matt. 28.9f. is implicitly ruled out by Luke 24.22–24, which tells of a visit of some disciples to the tomb in order to check on the assertions of these weak-minded females, who would no doubt have been better listened to, had they just seen the risen Lord; the christophany in Galilee recorded in Matt. 28.16–20 is replaced by a similar event in Jerusalem (Luke 24.36ff.), while the idea of a Galilean appearance is totally ignored.

Thus Luke's narrative is not based on its Matthaean counterpart, nor does Matthew's story of the sufferings and death of Jesus depend on Luke, as is also the case for the rest of the two gospels. Since neither of them even bothers to correct the other when there is a contradiction between them, it is clear that neither of the two evangelists had any knowledge of the book written by the other.[37]

But what about the relationship of the Lukan gospel to Mark? A

27

vast majority of scholars[38] think that Mark was one of Luke's two or three main sources and there is every reason to accept that theory. But does it apply to the Passion narratives in those gospels? Opinions on that point vary considerably, for a number of reasons.

To speak the language of elementary statistics, it is for instance striking that the Lukan Passion narrative should have only 27 per cent of its vocabulary in common with its Markan counterpart, whereas the rest of the third gospel, in the sections that have a Markan parallel, draws more than 50 per cent of its words from Mark, in spite of the well-known editorial activity of Luke.[39] Is it likely that Luke felt the need to rewrite the Markan Passion narrative much more thoroughly than the other parts of the gospel? Or is it not easier to account for the drastic reduction of common vocabulary in the Passion narrative if one assumes that Luke turned there to other sources than Mark rather more than he did in chs. 3–6, 8–9, and 18–21? A detailed analysis of the Lukan story of the sufferings and death of Jesus (chs. 22–24) will be necessary before we can answer those questions.

The transition from the apocalyptic discourse (Luke 21.5–36) to the first scene of the Lukan Passion narrative, which is the betrayal by Judas (22.3–6), is achieved by a fairly long summary of the activity of Jesus in the temple and of the reactions to it (21.37–22.2). This summary is largely editorial, of course, but it borrows bits of information from Mark 11 and 12, and from the unedited beginning of an independent Passion narrative which could be the Markan appendix or another, somewhat briefer in its introduction. As in the Matthaean parallel, the evangelist does his best to hide the seam between the Passion story and the description of Jesus' ministry in Jerusalem, ending with the apocalyptic discourse.[40] In other words, Matthew and Luke are both up against the same problem: the Passion narrative is not yet properly integrated to the gospel and they want to overcome that unsatisfactory state of affairs.

Luke offers no parallel to the episode of the anointing at Bethany (Mark 14.3–9), but tells elsewhere (Luke 7.36–50) a similar anecdote that took place in the house of a Pharisee by the name of Simon. Was the Bethany incident lacking in his source for the Passion narrative? This may have been the case, but it is not likely, since Luke objected to doublets and suppressed one of the forms of any narrative or saying which appeared twice in his sources.[41] Here, he seems to have opted for the longer form, which put the emphasis on forgiveness of sins – a favourite theme with him. He may also have found the anointing at Bethany rather pointless, since the women who went to the tomb meant to anoint Jesus' body as if the woman at Bethany had done nothing towards that.

The story of the betrayal by Judas directly follows the introduction, as a result of that cut (Luke 22.3–6). It is a good deal longer than its Markan parallel (Mark 14.10f.) and consists of one endless, clumsy sentence in which five successive clauses are connected artlessly with καί; the editorial contribution of Luke to this masterpiece of Greek prose was surely minimal, except perhaps in v. 3. As the verbal similarities with the Markan parallel are not particularly striking (19 of the 45 words of Luke are found in Mark, but the largest group of words existing on both sides consists of the last three words in Luke's v. 5) and as the style of Mark 14.10f. is a shade better than that of Luke 22.3–6, there is no reason to consider the former as the source of the latter. Thus they are two forms of the same story that have no direct literary relationship and both go back to an archetype.

The Lukan story of the Last Supper (22.7–38) begins with the episode of the preparation of the Paschal meal (vv. 7–14), which is a fairly close parallel to Mark 14.12–17. About 50 per cent of the words in Luke 22.7–14 are found in the Markan narrative and vv. 10–13 differ very little from Mark 14.13b–16. The natural conclusion would seem to be that Luke copied the Markan story and edited its beginning and its ending (vv. 7–9 and 14). But caution is needed, for various reasons. The Matthaean parallel (26.17–20), which had Mark as its only source and edited it drastically, borrows more than 60 per cent of its words from the Markan narrative; if Luke, whose redactional intervention concerned only four of the eight verses 22.7–14, shares only 50 per cent of its vocabulary with its Markan parallel, could that mean that he did not really start with the latter? Besides, even if the chronological remarks of Luke 22.7 and 22.14 may be editorial, there is no evidence that they certainly are; they could come from another continuous narrative of the Passion the chronology of which differed from that of Mark 14–16. Lastly, the Lukan story attributes the initiative of the preparation of the Passover to Jesus (v. 8), a feature unknown in the Markan and Matthaean parallels, but closely linked with Luke 22.15, where Jesus says to his disciples: 'It was my heart's desire to eat this Passover with you before I suffered.' Thus Luke 22.7–14 may come

for the most part from another Passion narrative, similar to Mark 14.
13b–16 in the middle section of the episode of the preparation of the
Passover and going its own way in telling the rest of the story.

The account of the meal (Luke 22.15–20) follows immediately,
which is the case neither in Mark, nor in Matthew, where the
prophecy of the betrayal precedes the supper. As is very well known,
the Lukan account differs widely from its counterpart in the first
two gospels. Of course, the shorter reading, which leaves out vv.
19b–20, is not well attested enough to be retained,[42] so that Luke
cannot be said to reverse the order of bread and cup found in I Cor.
11.23ff. and in the Markan and the Matthaean parallels.[43] But Luke
22.15–18 has no equivalent in the first two gospels, apart from Mark
14.25 and Matt. 26.29, which are distant parallels to Luke 22.18.
Those four verses offer a non-eucharistic, prophetic and eschatological interpretation of the Last Supper taken as a whole which is
vaguely similar to John 13.1ff. Verses 19 and 20, for their part, give
a sacramental meaning to the bread and to the cup. That is not
incompatible with the contents of vv. 15–18, since both paragraphs
insist on the prophetic sayings of Jesus uttered during the last meal
in order to prepare the disciples for their Master's death. It would
therefore be wrong to consider the combination of those two paragraphs as the result of late editorial work, done by the evangelist for
instance. It dates back a long way and was part of the Passion
narrative on which Luke based his chs. 22–24.

Some scholars maintain that Luke 22.19f. used Mark 14.22–24,
at least in part, as its source.[44] But the differences between the two
texts are numerous and far-reaching: the substitution of εὐχαρισ-
τήσας for εὐλογήσας in v. 19 and its implicit repetition in v. 20
(ὡσαύτως) are found also in I Cor. 11.24f. and therefore come from
a tradition other than the Markan one; the first addition after the
definition of the bread as 'my body' ('given for you') is symmetrical
with the phrase that follows the definition of the cup in the three
synoptic gospels, which makes it likely that it was produced in
tradition by the tendency to increase the symmetry between the
words on the bread and those on the cup;[45] the second addition ('do
this in remembrance of me'), exactly paralleled in I Cor. 11.24, also
originates in tradition; in v. 20, the actions of Jesus are simply
alluded to, as in I Cor. 11.25a, unlike Mark 14.23, a sure sign of two
different traditions, not of a shortening of the narrative by Luke;
the words of Christ differ extensively in the first half (Mark 14.24a

and Luke 22.20b), where Luke goes the way of I Cor. 11.25b when he says 'this cup' and 'the New Covenant', and become more similar in the second half (Mark 14.24b and Luke 22.20c), where the only difference is ὑπὲρ ὑμῶν in Luke instead of a more liturgical ὑπὲρ πολλῶν in Mark. This brief review of the differences between Luke 22.19f. and Mark 14.22–24 shows that both passages have the same structure, but diverge so much in detail that there is no literary relationship between them. Each of them is based on its own tradition and both traditions derive their common structure from the same archetype.[46]

Luke gives his version of the prophecy of the betrayal in 22.21–23, after the story of the meal itself, whereas Mark and Matthew place theirs before the latter. The Lukan version is shorter than the Markan one. Though 35 per cent of its words can be found in the Markan parallel, only the saying of v. 22 is really similar to its Markan counterpart. The order of the Lukan sayings and of the disciples' reaction, as well as the wording of vv. 21 and 23, are so different from what we read in Mark that Luke must be based on its own tradition. This tradition was certainly integrated into a longer unit, since there is no visible seam either at the beginning of v. 21 or at the end of v. 23. Since its theme is exactly the same as that of Mark 14.18–21 and since it is closely linked with the story of the last meal, as in Mark again, there is no doubt that there were two traditions of the Last Supper and surrounding episodes which had a common origin and had later diverged.

Luke 22.24–38, a collection of sayings uttered by Jesus in the upper room after the meal, can be called a Lukan farewell discourse. Its only parallel in the Markan Passion narrative is Mark 14.29f., which is fairly similar to Luke 22.33f., apart from the fact that it is located on the way to the Mount of Olives. Another parallel exists outside the Passion narrative: Mark 10.41–45 corresponds roughly to Luke 22.24–27. The other sayings in the collection (vv. 28–30, 31f., 35–38) have no parallel in Mark, but either have a counterpart in Matthew from Q (vv. 28–30 are related to Matt. 19.28) or sound very 'synoptic'. Thus, the best way to account for the presence of that Lukan farewell discourse is to admit that Luke felt the need for a solemn speech at this point and brought together several short sayings of Jesus which he arranged around the small nucleus of discourse (vv. 33f.) that pre-existed in the narrative of the Last Meal he made use of.

The Gethsemane scenes (Luke 22.39–53) follow, in the same order as in Mark. But both the prayer of Jesus and his arrest are told by Luke in his own way: the place name is changed to 'Mount of Olives'; the structure of the story of the prayer is much simpler, since Luke mentions neither the two groups of disciples nor the three successive prayers of Jesus which are a prominent feature of the Markan narrative; the story is a good deal shorter, in particular if Luke's vv. 43f., as is likely, do not belong to the original text of the gospel;[47] its vocabulary is quite different from that of Mark (only 26 per cent of the words are found in the Markan parallel and far less if one includes vv. 43f.); the story of the arrest (vv. 47–53) is also shorter than the Markan version; although its structure is the same as in Mark, a number of facts are different (Jesus prevents Judas from giving him a kiss; he heals the wound of the servant; his words just before being seized are more coherent, but leave out any reference to the fulfilment of scripture); its vocabulary shares only some 30 per cent of its words with the Markan parallel. On the other hand, the two stories are unmistakably the same in both gospels. It would be impossible to account for all the differences simply by Luke's editorial work. Thus, once again, we are led to assume that the traditions behind the two gospels were independent from each other, but were both derived from a common archetype, and that Luke made no use of the Markan narrative.

The trial before the high priest (22.54–71) then comes, as in Mark, without much transition – a sure sign that in tradition this story never existed apart from the account of the arrest. Although the various elements of the Markan narrative (gathering of the Jewish leaders, trial, ill-treatment, Peter's denial) all exist in Luke, the order of events and many of the details differ considerably there from what they are in Mark. Luke begins with the story of Peter's denial (vv. 54b–62), goes on to tell about the ill-treatment inflicted on Jesus, then mentions the gathering, which he places in the morning (v. 66), and finally gives his version of the trial (vv. 67–71), which does not include any allusion to the false witnesses who play a decisive part in Mark and Matthew. Within each of those four sections, Luke offers his own version of the events: I have dealt with Peter's denial earlier;[48] the gathering of leaders is postponed till morning, so that it can be a legal court session;[49] the ill-treatment takes place the night before and is attributed to the guards, not to the members of the Sanhedrin as is the case in Mark, at least partly; as for the trial itself, it consists mostly of a dialogue between the whole Sanhedrin and Jesus which expresses roughly the same ideas as the dialogue with the high priest in Mark, but does so quite differently. A sign of this is that, in spite of constant parallelism with Mark, only some 30 per cent of the words in Luke 22.54–71 are common to the two narratives. In short, if Luke had edited the Markan narrative here, it would be a very far-reaching editing job for which no real motive existed; it is therefore a better hypothesis to assume that the Markan and the Lukan texts are based each on its own tradition, both traditions going back to the same archetype, from which they diverged progressively.

The trial before Pilate (23.1–25), in the midst of which is inserted a trial before Herod (vv. 6–12) which has no counterpart in the other canonical gospels, is told, even apart from that parenthetical story, in a way which seldom coincides with the Markan narrative. The main features of the Lukan account are the political accusations launched against Jesus by the Jewish leaders (v. 2) and the triple attempt made by Pilate to free him, after having declared him to be innocent (vv. 13–16, 20, 22). Leaving aside the apologetic aspect of this attitude of the Roman governor, I want to stress the literary significance of this feature, which gives to this pericope a structure that has no counterpart in Mark. Only 17 per cent of the words used by Luke in that pericope are paralleled in the Markan story if we leave aside the Herod episode; if it is included, Luke's vocabulary is even less similar to Mark's, with only 12.6 per cent of its words found in the parallel. Those percentages make it impossible to claim that the Markan narrative here was the source of Luke. Luke may have edited more or less drastically the tradition he used, but it was no doubt a tradition that did not depend on Mark. This being said, the *dramatis personae* being the same, except for Herod, the situation being roughly identical and the outcome being in both texts the verdict of death against Jesus, the Markan and the Lukan traditions certainly go back to an archetype which told that story in a somewhat simpler fashion.

It is worth noting that Luke here makes no mention of the mocking of Jesus by the soldiers, a fact recorded at this juncture by the three other canonical gospels. Luke's silence on that aspect of the sufferings of our Lord is doubtless apologetic, and so editorial, since his double work is characterized by a constant tendency to show the attitude of the Roman authorities toward the disciples of Jesus in a favourable light.[50]

The story of the crucifixion (Luke 23.26–49) includes several anecdotes that are unknown to Mark and Matthew: the encounter with the women of Jerusalem on the road to Golgotha (23.27–31); the dialogue with the penitent thief (23.39–43); the repentance of the multitudes (23.48). The last of these may be editorial, as a preparation for the preaching of the apostles in Jerusalem according to Acts 2.36–39; 3.17–19; 4.8–12. The first two are more likely to be midrashic outgrowths of the Passion narrative, which may have become part of it before Luke inserted it into his gospel. In the parts of the story of the crucifixion that are common to Luke and Mark (13 verses out of 24 in Luke), there are striking differences: the name Golgotha vanishes in Luke; the words uttered by the various participants are all different, some wholly and others partly (see Luke's vv. 35b, 37, 46, 47b); the order of several episodes varies (see Luke's vv. 32, 33b, 36–38, 45), although the whole story is made up of a combination of roughly the same incidents; only some 38 per cent of the words of the Lukan version of the common parts are found in the Markan parallel. Some of those differences could be the result of an effort by Luke to rewrite Mark, but it is far more likely that the traditions behind the Markan and the Lukan narratives had already diverged from their common source, the archetype of the Passion story.

The scene of the burial of Jesus (Luke 23.50–55) is quite similar to the Markan story in essence, but diverges from it on a number of points: Joseph of Arimathaea is introduced at greater length (vv. 50f.); the reaction of Pilate is taken for granted (v. 52); the burial itself is described very briefly (v. 53 is much shorter than Mark's v. 46); the chronological note is placed after the burial (v. 54) instead of being the opening sentence of the pericope as in Mark, thus accounting for the hasty funeral rather than for the speedy request to Pilate; the names of the women who watched the burial are omitted, as they had been at the end of the crucifixion scene (v. 55; see also v. 49); 31 per cent of its words only are found in the Markan parallel. In short, it is the same story, but the two versions of it are too different for the one to be derived from the other. Even if Luke edited the tradition he used, as is likely, his text gives us an idea of what that tradition was like.

The story of the empty tomb (23.56–24.12) follows, as it does in

Mark. Although it does not differ radically from the Markan narrative, it has quite a number of features of its own. The women, who will be named only at the end of the narrative (v. 10a) instead of being introduced at the beginning, and who are not exactly the same as in Mark, prepare their 'spices and ointments' before the sabbath (23.56), not during the night that follows the sabbath (Mark 16.1). The fact of the tomb being open is simply mentioned (v. 2), whereas the Markan parallel elaborates on this unexpected miracle (Mark 16.3f.). The divine message is brought to them by two men (vv. 4–5a), not by a youngster. What those two angels have to say is mainly a reminder of Jesus' prophecy of his own Passion and Resurrection (vv. 5b–7), instead of being an assertion about Jesus' Resurrection followed by a message to deliver to the disciples. The women inform the apostles at once (vv. 9f.), but this is no use, since no one believes them (v. 11), so that their failure to convey the news of the Resurrection is as complete as in Mark, even though they behave better in Luke. Only 20 per cent of the words of Luke's narrative exist in the Markan parallel. Once again, it would be difficult to attribute all those differences to the editorial hand of Luke, even if it played its part. Luke made use of a tradition of his own, which was derived from the same archetype as the Markan parallel.

The stories of appearances of the risen Christ with which Luke's gospel ends (24.13–53) have of course no counterpart in Mark. They may be partly editorial, as is Matt. 28.16–20; this is the case for vv. 44–53. But some midrashic outgrowths of the Passion narrative are present in vv. 36–43 and a tradition unit of some size lies behind the story of the Emmaus disciples (vv. 13–35). As those narratives are completely different from the christophanies we read in Matt. 28 and John 20, apart from the fact that an appearance to the Eleven is found in each of these three gospels, the conclusion is that they were appended to the Passion narrative by Luke himself. It is worth noting that the *Sitz im Leben* of the tradition concerning the Emmaus disciples is liturgical; this poetic legend is meant to illustrate the idea of the eucharistic presence of the risen Christ.[51]

Our analysis of the Lukan Passion narrative thus comes to its end. It was evident throughout that its outline was roughly the same as that of its Markan parallel and that the story told here was, in spite of a number of divergences, the same one, since its chronology, its topography, its *dramatis personae*, its starting point, its progression and its concluding *coup de théâtre* all correspond almost exactly to their Markan counterparts. But at the same time it became clearer at every step that far-reaching differences existed between the Lukan and the Markan Passion narratives, in addition to the striking dissimilarity of their vocabulary. It is therefore not enough to assume that Luke made use of some isolated tradition units beside the Markan story, as this would account in no way for the fact that the differences are found in every single pericope to an extent which makes it highly unlikely that they might be purely editorial. The least we can do is to admit that Luke drew, not only on isolated tradition units (see 22.28–32, 35–38; 23.6–12; 24.13–35, 36–43), but also on a full account of the sufferings and death of Jesus that ran parallel to the Markan story.

The problem then arises whether Luke made use of two Passion narratives between which he chose at every point in the narrative. That would go against what a good judge, Henry J. Cadbury, considers to be his constant literary method,[52] that is to make his choice between sources every time he is confronted with two documents relating the same episode. If faced with two stories of the Passion, Luke would have opted for one of them and left the other aside altogether. The differences between his narrative in chs. 22–24 and Mark 14–16 are so great that he cannot be said to have opted in favour of Mark's story. Then he must have given preference to that other Passion narrative the text of which we know only through him.[53]

If Luke based his narrative in chs. 22–24 exclusively or almost exclusively on a Passion story other than the Markan one, two remarks have to be made. First, that long tradition unit must have been built on the same plan as Mark 14–16, apart from minor differences which we noticed as we were going through the narrative. The main divergences occur inside each pericope and have to do with the literary structure, the vocabulary and some details of it. In other words, the skeleton of the two Passion narratives found in church tradition is the same. The best way to account for that state of things is to assume that both were derived from an archetype which had a firm structure, but remained quite supple as far as the details of the narrative were concerned. That archetype of the Passion narratives existed before the traditions used by Mark and Luke started diverging. This takes us back a long time, well before AD 70 in any case.

Secondly, one may doubt whether Luke would have opted for another Passion narrative had he known the Markan one. Even though he claimed to have done better than his predecessors (Luke 1.1–4), including of course Mark, it is quite clear that he had the highest respect for Mark's book, in particular for the order of events, which he altered much less than Matthew. The Markan Passion narrative would no doubt have impressed him more than any other rival tradition, if he had known it, and he would have been bound to opt for it. It is therefore likely that he did not have any knowledge of it, because his copy of Mark's gospel did not include the appendix. Since his purpose was to write a history of salvation in his own time, beginning with John the Baptist and ending with Paul's missions, he was led to add to his main source, Mark, an Infancy narrative of John and Jesus and a Passion narrative that connected the account of Jesus' life with that of early Christian preaching as narrated in the first chapters of the book of Acts. In order to achieve his goal and write a continuous narrative, he had to resort to other traditions than the Markan gospel. One of those was his version of the Passion story.

5

The Passion narrative in John

The Passion narrative of the Fourth Gospel is the longest of all –
twice the size of its Markan counterpart. Its beginning and its end
are somewhat blurred, so that any precise statistics are impossible.
At one end, ch. 21 is not radically different from the christophanies
of ch. 20, but is doubtless a later addition[54] which should not be
included in the Passion narrative, whereas one may hesitate about
the scenes in 20.19–23 and 20.24–29. At the other end, the first episodes of the other Passion narratives are scattered and set in a different context in chs. 11–12 (the plot against Jesus in 11.47–53; the
anointing in Bethany in 12.1–8), while the Passion narrative as the
evangelist saw it begins in 13.1 with the story of the events that took
place on the occasion of the Last Supper.

Another somewhat disconcerting feature of the Johannine Passion
story is the fact that it has lost its character as a purely narrative
piece, owing to the extraneous nature of the Farewell Discourses
which extend from 13.12 to 17.26 and thus take up more than half
the length of the whole.

Finally, the style that prevails throughout the Passion narrative is
wholly Johannine. As the rest of the Fourth Gospel, that section was
entirely rewritten by the evangelist, even at places where a source or
a tradition can be perceived through his text. This writer or group
of writers leaves little evidence of the style and vocabulary of the
documents he uses.[55]

As a result of all those features, any reconstruction of the sources
or traditions behind the Johannine Passion narrative is highly
problematic. But let us not throw out the baby with the bath water.
If we take a close look at chs. 11–20 of the Fourth Gospel, we shall at
least be able to perceive some of the editorial adaptations made by

the evangelist, some of the motives behind them and something of the structure of the sources and traditions he used. As a matter of fact, we shall see that John's Passion narrative is a greatly edited form of a continuous story of the sufferings and death of Jesus built along the same lines as the synoptic narratives, but not, it seems, based on them.

The plot against Jesus (John 11.47–53) prepares the scene of his arrest (18.2–12). Although it differs greatly from its Markan counterpart (Mark 14.1f.), it plays the same part in the drama of Christ's Passion: the Jewish authorities reach a final decision to do away quickly with Jesus, who has become a menace. The reason why the writer of the Fourth Gospel brought it forward so much and thus separated it from the main body of the Passion narrative is quite clear: he wanted that plot to be a direct consequence of the raising of Lazarus from the dead (John 11.1–46), which thus became a striking symbol of the life-giving death of Jesus (see 11.6–16). The Master had died because he had given life to the man he loved.

The anointing at Bethany (12.1–8) follows after a brief interlude (11.55–57) the story of the plot against Jesus. It was deliberately placed there by the evangelist in order to preserve the connection with the plot (see vv. 4–8, particularly the attribution to Judas of the hostile remark about the woman's wasteful action) that existed in other Passion narratives, but even more so to establish a close link with the Lazarus episode (see vv. 1f. and 9–11) and with the triumphal entry into Jerusalem (12.12–18), which John considers as a consequence of the impression made on the crowd by the raising of Lazarus (see vv. 9–11 and 17f.) and as one more nail driven into the Master's coffin (see 11.57; 12.10f; 12.19).

As is usual with him, the fourth evangelist gives a new, fuller meaning to those episodes which he has in common with the synoptics. He achieves this by drastically rewriting the stories, without depriving them of their identity, and by placing them in what he considers to be the suitable context. If we take into account the fact that the context of 11.47–53 and 12.1–8 in chs. 11–12 is full of allusions of all sorts to the death of Jesus as an imminent event, we are justified in saying that to him these chapters were an introduction to the Passion narrative proper, which began with a solemn sentence in 13.1, followed by the Last Supper (13.2ff.). Thus, the evangelist built that ample introduction to the Passion around two episodes that were, in the same order, the first two pericopae in the Markan story of the sufferings and death of our Lord (Mark 14.1–9) and were followed after a short interval by the story of the Last Supper (Mark 14.17ff.). It is certainly not too bold to assume that he started from a continuous narrative of the Passion that began just like its Markan counterpart.

Did this tradition on the Passion include parallels to the pericopae of the betrayal by Judas (Mark 14.10f.) and the preparation of the Passover (Mark 14.12–16)? Although we cannot be sure, it might well be the case. John 13.26b–30 could be the Johannine equivalent of the betrayal episode. It shares the theme of Satan's entry into Judas' heart (v. 27a) with the betrayal pericope in Luke (Luke 22.3) and, in a highly Johannine fashion, attributes the initiative of that event to Jesus himself, who 'gives the morsel to Judas . . . and after the morsel, then Satan entered into him' (vv. 26b–27a). The last verse in that pericope (John 13.30) suggests that Judas goes out into the night in order to betray his Master. The betrayal itself does not have to be recorded, since it is as good as achieved once the supernatural powers that be have played their part about it. I may add that John 13.2, ambiguous though it is, probably means that Judas had made up his mind even before the Last Supper about betraying Jesus;[56] this allusion looks like a vestige of a pre-supper scene of betrayal similar to the one we find in the three synoptics.

If the preparation of the passover is missing in the Fourth Gospel, the reason is probably editorial. The evangelist wants it to be understood that Jesus was the Paschal Lamb, slaughtered on Passover eve (see 19.14, 29, 36) to 'take away the world's sin' (1.29; see also 1.36).[57] As a result, he has to suppress the only feature in tradition that connected the Last Supper with the Passover meal: the story of the preparation as it reads in the synoptics (Mark 14.12–16 and par.), with its many references to Passover eve and to the Passover supper, since the saying in Luke 22.15f. can be read as the expression of an unrealized wish.[58]

The story of the events that took place during the Last Supper begins at 13.1 and leads on to the Farewell Discourses (13.31–17.26), which are editorial for the most part and may have had a complex literary history (see for instance the last three words in 14.31, a well-known *crux interpretum*). The traditions the evangelist may have inserted into those long speeches[59] are very difficult to spot and cannot be reconstructed; but there is no reason to believe that they were attached to the Passion in any special way. There is no doubt that a large part of 13.1–30 is editorial too. But three elements found in that pericope correspond closely to what we find in the synoptic story of the Last Supper: the setting, which in both cases is an evening meal during which Jesus makes some strange gestures and utters some surprising words that have to do with his death; the theme of close association between the disciples and their Master (see John 13.8, 14); the announcement of the betrayal by one of the disciples (John 13.18f., 21–30). This suggests that the structure of the tradition on which John based his story was the same as that of Mark 14.17–25 and Luke 22.14–23. In other words, although no verbal parallelism exists, the synoptic and the Johannine traditions were similar enough to be derived from one archetype only.

After the episode of the last meal, including the Farewell Discourses, the synoptic parallels place the prayer of Jesus at Gethsemane (or the Mount of Olives, according to Luke). This is lacking in John, where we are not told what our Lord did in the garden beyond Kidron between his arrival there and his arrest (18.1ff.). But two facts suggest that the Master's prayer may have been recorded in the tradition used by the fourth evangelist: the Farewell Discourses end with a lengthy prayer of Jesus to his Father (17.1–26) which immediately precedes the story of the arrest (18.1–12); the theme of the synoptic prayer finds an echo in John 12.27, that is, in the editorial part of the introduction to the Passion narrative. The fourth evangelist objected to the all too human attitude of Christ drawing back for one moment from the terrible death he was facing, but he preserved the two features of that story which he felt were important: Jesus' emotion when his hour comes and his close union with his Father through prayer just before being separated from his disciples.

The story of the arrest of Jesus (18.1–12) differs from the synoptic accounts in a number of ways: the location (vv. 1f.); the part played by Judas, who acts as a guide and leader of the police party, but never manages to get near the Master (vv. 2f. and 5b–6); the composition of the police party (vv. 3 and 12a); Jesus' full mastery over the progression of events (vv. 4–5a, 6–8, 11); the disciples' escape arranged by Jesus, not left to their own initiative as in the synoptics (vv. 7–9); the identification of the one who draws the sword and of his victim as Peter and Malchus (v. 10); the allusion to Jesus' death as the cup he has to drink, which is further evidence for the suppression by the fourth evangelist of the prayer at Gethsemane, where this metaphor is central (v. 11b). But those differences are not enough to prevail over the similarities that exist between the synoptic and the Johannine accounts of the arrest: a garden beyond the river Kidron, where Jesus spends the night with his disciples; the arrival of an armed police party guided by Judas; a dialogue between Jesus and the people who came to arrest him; an isolated stroke of the sword by one of the companions of Jesus; the arrest of the Master alone, while the disciples get away. It is the same story. As no literary relationship seems to exist between its Markan, Lukan and Johannine forms,[60] we have to assume that these three narratives go back to one archetype, the structure of which they preserved.

The trial before the high priest follows (18.13–27), as in the synoptics, and is combined, also as in the other canonical gospels, with Peter's denial. Other similarities are: Jesus is brought to the house of a high priest in Jerusalem; Peter follows him, enters the courtyard of that house and warms himself by the fire lit by the servants there (vv. 15a, 16a, 16d, 18); Jesus is questioned by the high priest (v. 19) and makes an answer that is both proud and cautious (vv. 20f.); Peter denies his Lord (vv. 25–27a) and the cock crows (v. 27b). There is no doubt that this double narrative is basically the same in John, Mark and Luke; the intertwining of the two stories of Jesus and of Peter is too elaborate to have been invented by three independent writers. But the differences between John's narrative and those of Mark and Luke are none the less very extensive: the high priest to whose house Jesus is brought after his arrest is not Caiaphas, but his father-in-law Annas, a former holder of that office (v. 13); Peter is allowed into the courtyard only at the request of another disciple, who knew the high priest personally (vv. 15f.); he denies his Lord for the first time as he enters the courtyard (v. 17); no false witness is mentioned and the questioning of Jesus is done by the high priest, who does not seem to be surrounded by the members of the Sanhedrin (v. 19); the high priest's questions and Jesus' reply are quite different from what they are in the synoptics (vv. 19–21); Jesus is hit by a servant and objects to that ill-treatment immediately on replying, an incident only vaguely similar to the brutalities mentioned in the synoptic parallels (vv. 22f.); there is no verdict of any sort and Jesus is simply sent under guard by Annas to Caiaphas (v. 24). Part of those differences may be purely editorial (see vv. 14, 15f., 23), but many more no doubt go back to the tradition on which the evangelist based his narrative and make it impossible to claim that John had Mark or Luke as its source at this point. In short, the traditions behind those three gospels were not directly related, but all derived from a common archetype that was part of the continuous narrative which was the root of the three Passion stories.[61]

The trial before Pilate (18.29–19.16) is introduced, as in the synoptic parallels, by a brief note recording the fact that the Jewish authorities delivered Jesus to Pilate (18.28). The second half of this verse is editorial and aims at leaving no doubt in the reader's mind that the date of that fateful morning was the 14th of Nisan, i.e. Passover eve, so that the crucifixion, later that day, could be interpreted as the slaughter of the Paschal Lamb *par excellence*.

The story of the trial itself was drastically edited and thus acquired a typically Johannine style.[62] But behind this new face, it remains closely related to its synoptic counterparts. Jesus refuses to answer the accusations hurled at him by the Jewish leaders(vv. 34–36; see Mark 15.3–5 and Luke 23.9–10), but gives a guarded reply when Pilate asks him whether he is king of the Jews (vv. 37f.; see Mark 15.2 and Luke 23.3). The Barabbas episode follows, as in Mark and, if one leaves aside the trial before Herod, in Luke; although the Johannine version is the shortest of all, with two verses instead of six to nine verses in the synoptics, it contains the main ingredients of the story: the yearly Passover pardon, Pilate's offer to the people to grant it to Jesus, the riotous reaction of the crowd who want Barabbas freed, not Jesus (vv. 39f.). Then Jesus is scourged and mocked by the Roman soldiers (John 19.1–3), in the same order as in Mark – Luke having left out those events for apologetic motives. After the *Ecce homo* episode, which is the creation of the fourth evangelist (19.4–15), John concludes the trial before Pilate like the synoptics: Jesus is 'handed over to be crucified' (19.16a: see Mark 15.15b; Matt. 27.26b; Luke 23.25b). In other words, the Fourth Gospel tells here the same story as the synoptics, rather like Mark in places, more like Luke elsewhere. Once more, the best way to account for that state of things is to assume that John based his narration on a tradition which ran parallel to the ones used by Mark and Luke and had its origin in the same archetype of the Passion narrative.

The crucifixion is the next episode, in John (19.17–37) as in the synoptics. Two of the features common to Mark and Luke are missing in the Fourth Gospel: the drafting of Simon of Cyrene to carry the cross to Golgotha (Mark 15.21 and par.) and the mocking of Jesus on the cross by some at least of the people present (Mark 15. 29–32 and par.). Both passages could be considered as casting a doubt upon the absolute mastery of Jesus over himself and the situation around him, which made them objectionable in the eyes of John and accounts for their editorial suppression. A number of additional features characterize the Johannine narrative in comparison with the synoptics: reaction of the Jews to the *titulus* (vv. 20–22); further details about the sharing of Jesus' clothes by the soldiers (vv. 23f.); words addressed by Jesus to his mother and to the beloved disciple (vv. 25–27); piercing of the side of Jesus (vv. 31–37). They are all editorial, at least for the most part, and reinforce the Johannine traits of the narrative: the cross is the most complete manifestation of Jesus' glory, through the agency of Pilate (vv. 20–22); it is the fulfilment of many a scripture (vv. 23f., 33–37); the scene at the foot of the cross brings together Jesus' mother and beloved disciple, both highly symbolic figures in the Fourth Gospel (vv. 25–27); the piercing of Jesus' side probably has a deep symbolic meaning as well (see vv. 33–35).

If we leave aside those editorial suppressions and additions, the crucifixion episode follows the same pattern as its synoptic parallels, in spite of their different styles. Our Lord is taken to Golgotha and crucified there between two thieves (vv. 17f.); a *titulus* is placed on the cross and calls him 'the king of the Jews' (v. 19); the soldiers share Jesus' clothes (vv. 23f.); some women who had been among his followers are present (v. 25); after uttering a last word and being given a drink of vinegar, Jesus expires (v. 28–30), a fact vouched for by the soldiers (vv. 32f.). This fairly complex story, in which several individuals and groups play a part, is too similar to its synoptic counterparts to be unrelated to them. But its vocabulary is so different (only 15 per cent of its words in the verses paralleled in Mark have a Markan counterpart) and so many details diverge in the common sections (the chronology; the description of Jesus' clothes; the location of the group of women; the suppression of the three hours of darkness and of the tearing in two of the temple veil; the words of Jesus; the suppression of the centurion's confession; etc.) that none of the synoptic parallels is likely to have been John's source. Once again, the only way to account for the relationship between the various Passion narratives is to assume that they go back to the same archetype, from which they diverged each in it own way.

The burial of Jesus comes next (19.38–42), as in the synoptic parallels. The story is roughly the same: the request of Joseph of Arimathaea to Pilate, who grants it (v. 38); the body of Jesus is attended to (v. 40) and buried in some haste (v. 42). But the Johannine pericope leaves out the mention of the women found in Mark 15.47 (and par.) and adds several features that give it a special flavour: the part played by Nicodemus (v. 39); a crude embalming of the body of Jesus (v. 40); the location of the tomb in a garden near Golgotha (v. 41). All those additions are editorial and connected with other features of the Fourth Gospel (3.1ff.; 20.1, 15).

The story of the discovery of the empty tomb follows, as in Mark and Luke (John 20.1–13). It has a number of original features, which may not all be editorial: Mary Magdalene alone goes to the tomb on the Sunday morning (v. 1); on finding the stone removed from the tomb, she runs away and reports at once to Peter and the Beloved Disciple (v. 2); they rush to the tomb and see; the latter believes and they go away (vv. 3–10); then the woman sees two angels in the tomb and exchanges a few words with them (vv. 11–13). The special part played by Mary Magdalene here corresponds to her being mentioned first in the lists of women at the tomb in the synoptics (Mark 16.1 and par.) and probably derives from tradition, as do also the two angels in the tomb. The rest, in particular vv. 3–10, is John's contribution.

From the pericope of the discovery of the empty tomb, which has even less of an ending than in Mark, John moves on to several stories of appearances of the risen Christ (20.11–29), which I shall not analyse here, apart from noting that they have no visible relationship with the ones in Matthew and Luke. The theme of vv. 14–18 is somewhat similar to that of Matt. 28.9; vv. 19–23 satisfy the same need as Matt. 28.16–20 and Luke 24.36–43. But what we have here is a purely artificial group of pericopae, some editorial and some based on the tradition of this or that church, which have no literary link between them and were appended to the Passion narratives when these were inserted into gospels. The traditional Passion narratives used by the fourth evangelist thus ended, like the Markan one, with the discovery of the empty tomb.[63]

In short, the author of John's Gospel used as his source for chs.

11–20 a continuous Passion narrative that had exactly the same limits, the same narrative thread and the same stories as those used by Luke and by the redactor who appended a story of the sufferings and death of Christ to the original Gospel of Mark. Whether John borrowed that Passion narrative from one, two or three of the synoptic gospels remains at this point a possibility, but seems most unlikely at first glance, owing among other factors to the far-reaching differences between the christophanies of the various gospels – differences which would have been reduced if the Fourth Gospel had known Matthew or Luke. It is wiser to assume that John had at his disposal, like Luke before him, a Passion narrative derived from an archetype that was also at the root of the Lukan and the Markan stories of the sufferings and death of Christ.

This being granted, my next task will be to try and find out what such an archetype of the Passion narratives was.

PART II

THE OLDEST CHRISTIAN
LITURGY OF ALL

6

A mere record of facts?

It is clear from what was said earlier that, if the Matthaean Passion narrative is based on its Markan parallel, the latter and its Lukan and Johannine counterparts are all independent from one another, as well as from Matthew. To account for the striking similarities between those three independent stories of the last two or three days in the life of Jesus, I suggested that we had to assume the existence of a common archetype from which the three traditions leading to the narratives in the canonical gospels were derived at an early stage.

As I showed in chapter 2 about Mark 14–16, and in chapter 5[64] about John 11–12, the traditions in question were continuous narratives, not isolated units which the evangelists had to thread together. The only question that remained open was whether the episodes preceding the arrest of Jesus had had an independent existence, since some of them were well-rounded anecdotes (anointing in Bethany, Last Supper) and a fairly satisfactory *Sitz im Leben* could be imagined for two or three of them (anointing, Supper, prayer at Gethsemane). It is now time to settle that matter.

The anointing in Bethany of course has a fairly close parallel in Luke 7.36–50, which was doubtless an isolated unit of tradition. But the lesson drawn by Jesus from the same act is quite different there from what it is in the context of the Passion narrative in Matthew, Mark and John. As a matter of fact, the message of the Master in Luke 7.40–47 gives a generally applicable meaning to the wild gesture of the woman and makes it an excellent illustration of the theme of repentance and forgiveness of sins, whereas Jesus' words in Mark 14.6–9 and parallels point towards the death and burial of our Lord and interpret the woman's wasteful action as an acted prophecy of those events which belongs naturally to a Passion narrative, side by side with the story of the last meal. Add to this the fact that such an example of lavish spending for worship is not likely to have been proffered in the early Jerusalem church, where the poor and the sharing of wealth with the brethren were the absolute priorities (see Acts 1–6), whereas it was an edifying memory well worth recalling in the framework of an extended story of the sufferings and death of Christ. One may even venture the hypothesis that the tradition underlying Luke 7.36–50 was borrowed from the Passion narrative and used as a separate 'paradigm' – as Dibelius would have called it[65] – in the preaching of a later, richer Hellenistic church, where almsgiving, lavishness in worship and sentimentality could easily be combined.

The story of the Last Supper is not as clearly limited and as neatly centred around a saying of Jesus as the anointing, since there are three or four different sub-stories within it (preparation, prophecy of the betrayal, sayings on the bread and the cup, plus the farewell discourse in two of the gospels). But it is quoted by Paul in I Cor. 11.23–26 as the normative text for the organization of the Eucharist and this communal meal could be described as the *Sitz im Leben* of a tradition unit consisting of that story or part of it. The difficulty is that the sayings of Jesus here all point towards the dangers that menace his life and towards his tragic death (see Mark 14.13f., 18, 20f., 22, 24f. and par.). In particular, the eating and drinking of the disciples is interpreted as an acted prophecy of their Master's death,[66] just as was the case with the anointing. It is thus most likely that the whole story of the Last Supper was a part of the Passion narrative as soon as it came into being. What Paul was quoting from in I Cor. 11.23–26 was not a tradition on the Last Supper; it was the Passion narrative in a form closely similar to the Lukan story.

As for the prayer at Gethsemane, it could be seen as an example of submissiveness in prayer. Its *Sitz im Leben* would then be the teaching of the church. But can this episode be separated from the arrest, which follows immediately? Can it be read without the story of the sufferings and death, which alone accounts for the deep spiritual crisis that Jesus is shown to undergo at this point? I do not think so. Having described two prophetic gestures which sealed the fate of Jesus, the Passion narrative adds here an episode that was still needed before the tragedy could begin: Christ's assent to his own death and the disciples' inability to share in their Master's sufferings.

In short, none of the episodes that precede Jesus' arrest in the Passion narrative is likely to have been a separate unit of tradition, so that our quest of an archetype applies to the whole story as told in the canonical gospels.

Three main hypotheses have been offered to account for the origin and nature of this first story of the sufferings and death of our Lord: a mere record of the facts, based on the memories of eyewitnesses; a kind of *midrash* based on a limited number of proof-texts and identifying Jesus with the Suffering Servant or the Righteous Sufferer; an expanded form of the early Christian *kerygma* as we know it from Paul's quotation in I Cor. 15.3ff. I shall examine these three theories and try to show why they ought to be rejected, before I turn to another hypothesis which I take to be far more satisfactory than they are, in spite of the small number of scholars who defend it: that of a liturgical origin of the archetype of the Passion narratives as we have them in the canonical gospels.

Let us begin with the hypothesis that considers the original Passion narrative as a mere record of facts. It has its attraction, since our three independent stories of the sufferings and death of Christ give us an account of the same events along roughly similar lines and do not offend greatly against likelihood in spite of their being written half a century or more after the facts. Whether written or oral, such a record would have been based on the memories of eyewitnesses and its outline would be likely to be modelled on the actual succession of events. Thus, on all the points where the three Passion narratives agree, we would stand a good chance of being near the facts.

To take but a few examples, the Passion narratives agree on a fairly accurate description of the religious situation that existed in and around Jerusalem about AD 30.[67] What is said there about the Passover celebrations, with their vast gathering of pilgrims, the Jerusalem Sanhedrin, the high priest Caiaphas and his father-in-law and predecessor Annas may be ambiguous or faulty at some points, but on the whole is correct. The political set-up which we know reasonably well through Josephus is assumed as the back-drop of the arrest, trial and execution of Jesus: a stiff Roman military rule with a constant readiness to use force in order to prevent disorder, the sending of reinforcements headed by the governor himself to Jerusalem at the time of the Passover pilgrimage, the residual authority granted to the high priest inside the temple and in the Jerusalem area, etc.[68] The judicial system alluded to in the Passion narratives is not precisely described, but reasonably well understood, with its co-existence of the Jewish Sanhedrin, judging by the Law of Moses, and the governor's court, where the verdicts are based on the limitless *imperium* of the occupying power and where capital punishment takes the form of crucifixion.[69] The topography suggested in the Passion narratives is not clear on all points, but it makes sense when compared with the geography of the area and what we know of its place names.[70]

Over-exaggerated scepticism as to the historical likelihood of the events thus recorded should therefore be avoided. But it would be naïve to imagine that the Passion narratives or their common archetype are a plain record of events as they took place and were witnessed by well-informed, trustworthy and intelligent people. There are the difficulties.

We need not be bothered at this point by the problem raised by the idea of resurrection from the dead from the historian's point of view. What the narrators recorded, here as everywhere else, was not 'brute facts', but the impression some events had made on the people present. If these people believed resurrection was a possibility through an act of God and felt sure they had witnessed one, that uncritical understanding of the facts went straight into the narratives. We should not look for intermediate stages at which supernatural events would have been introduced into the story as a later development. Even if resurrection remains a problem for the historian, it is nothing of the sort for the literary critic who simply tries to find out what the oldest form of the Passion narrative was.

The difficulties arising from the hypothesis that it was a mere record of facts based on eyewitness evidence are none the less real. First, some at least of the episodes of the Passion took place in circles or localities to which no disciple could gain access or was likely to have been present: the Master's prayer at Gethsemane, the trials before the high priest and before Pilate, the crucifixion are good examples of this. Those events are none the less recorded in the same style as the other events, that is, with a clear bias in favour of Jesus. In other words, scenes directly reported by eyewitnesses and scenes known in an indirect way were evened up into a continuous narrative which can hardly be described as a mere record of facts since it is the product of a fairly complex literary process.[71]

Besides, some of the events recorded in the Passion narratives raise difficult questions of various kinds. To take a few examples, is the

very quick succession of episodes which is so noticeable a feature of
the four Passion stories compatible with the idea that they are based
on a mere record of facts? From the Last Supper to the burial of
Jesus, less than twenty-four hours elapse; in spite of their chronological differences, the synoptics and the Fourth Gospel agree on
this. The arrest of Jesus takes place in the night following the Last
Supper; the high priest delivers his prisoner to Pilate very early the
next morning; Jesus is crucified that same morning and dies on the
cross in the afternoon of that day; he is buried before night falls.[72]
When it is remembered that a court session of the Sanhedrin was not
supposed to take place during the night or during a feast-day,
especially if the life of a man was at stake; that the distances from
one point to another in and around Jerusalem were not negligible;
that the death-struggle of people condemned to die on the cross
was usually a very slow one, etc., it becomes evident that doubts
are bound to arise as to the likelihood of that chronology. Is it enough
to speak of a hasty trial and of the quick death of an exhausted
Jesus? Certainly not. Here is a major problem for the historians, who
are wrestling with possible solutions.[73] Even though this difficulty is
not as insuperable for us, since our approach is a literary one, it
makes it very doubtful whether the earliest Passion narrative can be
described as a mere record of facts. This archetype of the canonical
narratives for some reason crammed a number of events into an
incredibly narrow chronological framework. By doing so, its author
showed that his goal was not to write a plain chronicle, but to
interpret the facts.

Then there is the problem of the legal procedure used in sentenc-
ing Jesus to death. Things are reasonably clear as far as the Roman
trial is concerned: an expeditious court hearing chaired by the
governor, then a flogging and finally an execution by crucifixion.
There is nothing strange or unlikely in that narrative, apart from the
Barabbas episode, particularly if it is referred to as an application of
a yearly custom (see Mark 15.6 and par.) unknown from other
evidence.[74] That is not enough to cast doubt on the historical validity
of this part of the Passion narratives, which could be considered as a
reasonably good record of the facts. But the story of the Jewish trial
is a different case. As I said earlier, the hasty meeting of the Sanhedrin in the middle of the night as recorded in Mark 14.55ff. and
Matt. 26.59ff. is hard to reconcile with what we know of the pro-
ceedings of Jewish courts in those days, even if it was followed by

another session in the early morning, as Mark 15.1 and Matt. 27.1 suggest.[75] Luke's morning session of the Sanhedrin (22.66ff.) raises fewer objections, but remains an anomaly, since it is held on a feast-day. John's story (18.13ff.) leaves no room for a meeting of the Sanhedrin and only mentions the questioning of Jesus by Annas, a former high priest, during the night and a brief detention of the prisoner by the high priest Caiaphas at the end of the night (18.24, 28); that version of the Jewish 'trial' is far more satisfactory from a legal point of view and might be based to some extent on eyewitness evidence (see John 18.15f.). But it looks like a conscious attempt at improving the original narrative retained in two different forms by the Synoptists. Thus, the archetype certainly gave a distorted view of the facts of the Jewish trial of Jesus for reasons which I shall try and discover later.[76]

It has become quite clear why the archetype of the Passion narratives cannot have been a mere record of facts. But this should not lead us to deny to it the features of a narrative. Human life is made up of so many events of all kinds and sizes that a mere record of facts is impossible and would in any case not be manageable. In order to use it as the subject matter of literature, writers have to select some of those facts and put them together in the order they choose. If they opt for the narrative form, that order will be dictated to them by chronological, topographical and logical reasons, but their selection of facts will result from their own view of things and therefore will tend to vary from person to person. Since the three independent Passion narratives record roughly the same events, we can be sure that they derive from the same narrative and accept its selection of facts as their starting point. Since they differ very little between them as to the order of episodes, there is every reason to think that the events selected by the author of the archetype were organized into a continuous narrative with a strong literary structure, which it would have been difficult to take to pieces.

In other words, the archetype of the Passion narratives was based on a selection of facts known from various sources and chosen for reasons as yet undecided. It was a continuous and reasonably coherent narrative arranged in an order dictated by the logic of narration and by its *Sitz im Leben* and the practical use it was put to.

7

A midrash?

It was sometimes suggested that the earliest Passion narrative was not a report based on eyewitness evidence, but a collection of stories told *à propos* a number of Old Testament proof-texts foretelling the sufferings and death of the Righteous One, the Servant of the Lord or the Messiah.[77] In other words, the nucleus of it all would have been a group of *testimonia* concerning the martyrdom of God's Elect One and the narrative would have arisen as *midrash pesher* – Qumran-wise – or simply *midrash* of the *testimonia*, in order to show how those prophecies had been finally fulfilled in Jesus' Passion.

It may seem surprising to consider a narrative as an illustrative commentary on a collection of Old Testament texts. But *midrashim*, a well-known *genre* in those days, were made up of stories that were both an expansion and a commentary of biblical books, while *pᵉsharim* applied the contents of the writings of Old Testament prophets to the life of the Teacher of Righteousness and to the history of the Qumran community, considered as their eschatological fulfilment.[78] Besides, the existence in some Jewish circles of the last two centuries BC and of the first century AD of collections of proof-texts concerning this or that major theological theme, once a brilliant conjecture, has now been fully demonstrated.[79] Thus, there is nothing strange in trying to define the Passion narrative as an eschatological *midrash* of prophecies announcing the sufferings and death of the Elect of God.

Another justification of that understanding of the Passion narrative is the fact that *testimonia*, which are well attested in early patristic literature, such as the Epistle of Barnabas and the writings of Justin Martyr,[80] have left a number of traces in the New Testament. A few examples will be enough. When Paul quotes the *kerygma* of the early

Jerusalem church in I Cor. 15.3ff., two of the statements in this authoritative tradition are followed by the words κατὰ τὰς γραφάς (in accordance with the scriptures): that Christ died for our sins and that he was raised on the third day. This is a well-known *crux interpretum*, since no one really knows what these scriptures might be.[81] A likely explanation is that they are collections of proof-texts read as prophecies of those two events. The end of Paul's speech to King Agrippa (Acts 26.22f.) states that the speaker never said anything else than what the prophets and Moses had foretold: 'whether the Christ must suffer, whether he, the first out of the resurrection of the dead, will announce light to the people and to the Gentiles.' These two unconnected clauses, related somewhat clumsily by an εἰ to the verb describing the proclamation of Moses and the prophets (ἐλάλησαν), sound just like the headlines of two chapters in a collection of messianic *testimonia*.[82] It will have become clear to everyone that the subject matter of those two chapters would have been the same as that presupposed by the double κατὰ τὰς γραφάς of the *kerygma* as quoted in I Cor. 15.3ff. This makes it very likely indeed that the early Christian preachers and teachers had collections of *testimonia* at their disposal and that the themes of the sufferings, death and resurrection of Christ were central in these collections. Another example can be added: Heb. 1.5–14, where a chain of Old Testament quotations concerning God's Son is inserted in the author's demonstration of Jesus' superiority over the angels. The theme here is different, but remains christological. In other words, there is no doubt that the early Christian church made use of christological *testimonia* from the Old Testament and that some of these were collections centred on the themes of the sufferings, the death and the resurrection of Christ.

Could such a collection or a grouping of them have been the original nucleus of the Passion narrative? What makes this a possibility worthy of discussion is the fact that biblical allusions and quotations are numerous in the canonical Passion narratives. Of course, some of those allusions and quotations were added by the evangelists at the time of the redaction of each of the gospels. The best instance of this is the additional scriptural material that appears in the Matthaean Passion narrative: a quotation in Matt. 27.9f.; allusions in Matt. 26.15 and 27.34, 43. The first two of those four came with the midrashic expansions concerning Judas which Matthew added to the Markan story in Matt. 27.3–10 and 26.15.

The third and fourth are learned contributions made by the evangelist, as I showed earlier.[83] The same origin is likely in the case of the two scripture quotations that conclude the Johannine story of the piercing of the side of Jesus (John 19.31–37).

But by far the largest number of Old Testament quotations and allusions in the Passion narratives of the canonical gospels are so well integrated into the fabric of the story that they cannot have been added later by Christian scholars. In the Markan story, out of some twenty-five allusions to Old Testament texts, one only is a formal quotation from scripture, with a proper introduction ($\gamma\acute{\epsilon}\gamma\rho\alpha\pi\tau\alpha\iota$). The others hardly show at all, apart from the transcription of the Aramaic cry of the dying Master (Mark 15.34 and the Matthaean parallel), which is a quotation from Ps. 22.2, but does not present itself as scripture. Only the well trained eye or ear can recognize the words of Old Testament writers. It is as though the texts had remained in the background and their narrative commentary had become a separate entity, with a few words from the texts here and there.

If we could be sure of the contents of the collection or collections of *testimonia* serving as a nucleus of the original Passion narrative, the case for this attractive hypothesis would be fairly strong. Unfortunately, we do not possess that information. All we can do is to start from the allusions to this or that text in the narrative and to try and reconstruct a list of the scripture passages selected as proof-texts. But it is a difficult task and the result is rather disappointing at first sight, since there seems to be little order and unity in that list. At close scrutiny, some interesting facts appear. For instance, about one in every five of the Old Testament allusions found in the Markan story refers to the last hymn of the Suffering Servant of the Lord in Isaiah 53 (Mark 14.24, 49b, 61; 15.4f., 27), while two more suggest Isa. 50.6, which is part of another of these hymns (Mark 14.65 and 15.19). About one in every three of those allusions refers to the Psalms of David (Mark 14.3c, 18, 34, 56, 62b; 15.24, 29, 34, 36), the most frequently mentioned of these being Ps. 22, which occurs three times in the relatively brief pericope of the crucifixion (Mark 15.24, 29, 34). But no other pattern is visible in the distribution of scriptural allusions.

How are we to account for this complex state of affairs? This is not the place for a full discussion of the difficult problem of 'the Bible of the early Church'.[84] Even if first-generation Christianity had selected some chapters and groups of chapters in the Old Testament as their special Canon and if one of the sections of that Canon was centred on the theme of the Suffering Servant,[85] the distribution of scriptural allusions in the Passion narratives is too erratic to encourage their readers to believe that their archetype was a midrashic commentary on the fifteen or so chapters of the books of Isaiah and of Psalms brought together into the relevant section. If we think in terms of collections of *testimonia* made up of short quotations never longer than a few verses, it becomes difficult to imagine what the order of that collection was, since the biblical allusions in the Passion narratives have almost no continuity and seldom concern the same book twice in succession, while the themes vary from one allusion to the next.

In other words, the hypothesis of a midrashic origin of the Passion narrative, attractive though it be, fails to account for the part played by biblical quotations and allusions in the four canonical versions of that story.

But some of the facts we mentioned when analysing the scriptural references in the Markan narrative still require an explanation. There is first the large number of allusions to the Servant hymns of Deutero-Isaiah, to which the Lukan Passion adds at least one (Luke 22.37) and possibly two (if Luke 23.34 is authentic, which is doubtful) references to Isa. 53.12. Those allusions are totally integrated to the narrative and scattered from the Last Supper to the crucifixion, at the rate of one in each major pericope. This discreet presence suggests that the hymns were not perceived as proof-texts for the sufferings and death of Christ, but were none the less read by the early Christians as a prophecy of the Passion.[86] Although the Passion narrative can in no case be considered as a *midrash* of those hymns or of the last of them, the evidence being far too slight for that conclusion, it could be said to bear the mark of the narrator's interest in those telling meditations on the fate of the Suffering Servant of the Lord. Some details in the story of Jesus' sufferings and death were, it seems, suggested by the texts of Deutero-Isaiah: the Lukan dialogue about the two swords (Luke 22.35–38), as well as the description of the men crucified with Jesus as thieves (Mark 15.27 and par.), refer to the 'he was numbered with transgressors' of Isa. 53.12; the silence of Jesus when accused, as in Mark 14.61a and 15.4f. (and par.), reminds one strongly of the double 'he opened not his mouth' in Isa. 53.7 and would probably not have been mentioned were it not for that feature of the last hymn of the Servant of the Lord; the description of the ill-treatment inflicted on Jesus (Mark 14.65 and 15.19 and par.) is reminiscent of Isa. 50.6 and may have been based on that text. Thus some features of the original Passion narrative were probably borrowed from Deutero-Isaiah.

As we noted earlier, the allusions to the Psalms of David are by far the largest group of references to scripture in the Markan Passion narrative. Both Matthew (27.34, 43) and Luke (23.49) added to this pre-eminence of the book of Psalms. The allusions to the Psalms are scattered far and wide before the episode of the trial before the high priest, where there are two (Mark 14.56, 62b), then are absent during the trial before Pilate and finally are clustered together in the pericope of the crucifixion (Mark 15.24, 29, 34, 36 and par.; Matt. 27.34, 43; Luke 23.49) and are missing in the episodes of the burial and of the empty tomb. The ten or so Psalms alluded to in the synoptic narratives have little unity and no pattern is visible in this distribution. All we can say is that the narrator found inspiration in the Psalms and probably borrowed this or that detail of his narrative from them: the idea of an anointing of the *head* of Jesus (Mark 14.3c and par.) may come from Ps. 23.5, since it is associated with the idea of enemies being near both in the Psalm and in the gospels; Mark 14.18c certainly alludes to Ps. 41.10 when it calls the traitor 'the one who eats bread with me', a description which Matthew left out because he found it unnecessary; the words of Jesus speaking to his disciples in Gethsemane (Mark 14.34 and Matt. 26.38) before he goes aside to pray are clearly reminiscent of Pss. 42.6, 12 and 43.5, a hymn of despair and hope in God which may have helped to mould the Markan story around three prayers of Jesus; the answer given by Jesus to the high priest (Mark 14.62 and par.) includes an allusion to Ps. 110.1 which is combined in an intriguing way with one to Dan. 7.13 and contributes the messianic dimension to what would otherwise simply be an eschatological prophecy, thus accounting for the high priest's question as recorded in v. 61b; etc. In other words, an early church that constantly read the Psalms of David was influenced by some of them in the process of elaboration of a tradition telling the story of the Passion, to the extent of structuring some episodes or enlarging some after models found in the Psalms. This is of course quite different from the hypothesis of a midrashic origin of the Passion narrative and means a much looser contact between the editorial work and this or that biblical book or collection of proof-texts.

But does this apply to the crucifixion narrative, where, as I said earlier, the allusions to the Psalms, particularly to Ps. 22, are unusually numerous and visible? We must keep in mind that eye-witness evidence for that scene was no doubt scanty or even non-existent, as the evangelists themselves allow, if we leave John aside, since they report that the only companions of Jesus who saw some-thing of their Master's execution were some women who watched it 'from afar' (Mark 15.40 and par.). The crucifixion having quickly become one of the main themes of Christian preaching, as the missionary speeches in Acts and the epistles of Paul show, some kind of a narration of it was an absolute necessity as a chapter of a story of the whole Passion. Hence the tendency of the original narra-tor and of later redactors and evangelists to turn to Psalms describing in the first person singular the anguish and hope of the persecuted believer (Pss. 22, 69 and 109) or at least of man in the throes of God's wrath (Pss. 38 and 88), in order to find in those inspired poems prophecies which the death of Jesus on the cross had fulfilled. It would be an exaggeration to say that the crucifixion narrative arose as a *midrash pesher* of Ps. 22, since there are after all only three reasonably clear allusions to that Psalm in the Markan version of that episode, that is, in a pericope twenty verses long. But it is not too much to assume that the narrator of this scene had Ps. 22 in mind, and probably Ps. 69 as well, and that it was customary in first-century Christian churches to associate these Psalms and others with the memory of the crucifixion in a special way.[87]

That is all we can retain of the hypothesis of a midrashic origin of the Passion narrative.

8

An expanded form of kerygma?

The word *kerygma*, 'proclamation', is not very common in the New Testament, where the corresponding verb, κηρύσσειν, and a near-synonym, εὐαγγέλιον, occur much more often (61 times the former, 76 times the latter, as against eight occurrences of κήρυγμα,[88] mostly in the Pauline epistles). But it has become a favourite among theologians of the New Testament in our century as a designation of early Christian preaching to outsiders. Its precise meaning varies considerably from scholar to scholar.[89] I shall use it here as the name for a brief summary of the Christian message about Jesus Christ centring on the sufferings, death and resurrection of our Lord such as we find in I Cor. 15.3ff. and at the core of most of the missionary speeches recorded in the book of Acts (see Acts 2.23f., 36; 3.13–15; 4.10–12; 5.30f.; 10.40, 42; 13.27–30.[90] Such summaries belonged to authoritative church tradition and probably go back a long way towards the beginnings of Christian missionary enterprise.

Since the various versions of the *kerygma* all concur in being a crisp enumeration of facts with a few words of theological comment at most, it is not surprising that some scholars should have compared them with the Passion narratives, in which the same events are also central and the narrative is left to speak for itself with few interpretative remarks only. This comparison led some of those scholars to consider the *kerygma* as the original nucleus of the Passion narrative, to which the growth of tradition added little by little a number of stories concerning the events simply listed in the early summary of Christian preaching.[91] Ever since Rudolf Bultmann attached his name to that hypothesis, it has found firm advocates in all schools of thought among New Testament specialists, including conservatives who have little in common with him otherwise.[92]

If one leaves aside the differences between the various exponents of that hypothesis, it can be summarized as follows: the half dozen short sentences of the *kerygma* gave birth to a brief continuous narrative three or four times longer; that brief narrative in its turn blossomed into a number of anecdotes which remained attached to its main thread; finally, isolated tradition units that had grown separately, like the story of the anointing in Bethany, the prophecy of the betrayal, the Last Supper, the prayer in Gethsemane and Peter's denial, were attached to the continuous narrative, that had continued in the meantime producing new shoots, such as the story of the preparation of the Passover meal, the trial before the high priest and the questioning by Herod. This is an attractive allegory of growth which tries at the same time to account for the unevennesses and seams than can be detected in the Passion narratives and first of all in its Markan form.

But those unevennesses and seams are not as numerous and as striking as some scholars say. The best example of an over-emphasis on those difficulties is Rudolf Bultmann's *History of the Synoptic Tradition*.[93] There is simply no evidence that Mark 14.10f. should follow immediately 14.1f., so that 14.3–9 should be considered as a later addition; pericopae describing the plot against Jesus alternate all through Mark 14 with pericopae showing Jesus' mastery over the events (Mark 14.1f., 10f., 18–21, 43–52 on one side; Mark 14.3–9, 12–17, 22–42) and this pattern shows no sign of being superimposed on an earlier narrative. It simply does not do to assert dogmatically that Mark 14.8f. was appended to an apophthegm ending with vv. 6f. which had no connection with the Passion; a phrase like 'but you will not always have me' (14.7c) certainly points towards Jesus' death and leads on to vv. 8f., which complement – and in no way contradict – the lesson drawn by the Master in vv. 6f. from the woman's action. The story of the Last Supper (Mark 14.12–25) raises many problems,[94] but the fact that the words 'while they were eating' occur in v. 18 and in v. 22 is no proof that vv. 17–21 and 22–25 did not originally belong to the same pericope; it simply shows that the narrator wanted to record two sets of remarks made by Jesus during the meal. As for the lack of any mention of the paschal lamb in vv. 22–25, taken as evidence that a Hellenistic cult legend here replaces the original story of the Passover meal, it merely suggests that the narrator was interested only in the acts of the disciples interpreted by their Master as prophecies of his death; to conjecture the substitution of one story for another on that slender basis can only be described as wild. In order to prove that the pericope of the prayer in Gethsemane (Mark 14.32–42) was originally a completely independent story, it is not enough to point to the fact that v. 26 says that Jesus and his disciples went to the Mount of Olives, while v. 32 mentions their arrival in the garden of Gethsemane; as so many people have been naïve enough to believe, the narrator may perhaps have assumed that Gethsemane was located somewhere on or near the Mount of Olives. That list of exaggerated conclusions derived from flimsy evidence could easily be extended. But it would get rather monotonous and I prefer to stop at this point. What matters is to be aware of the weakness of a method based on constant and arbitrary denial of the existence of even the most visible narrative patterns in what has first been described as a continuous story set in a strong frame.

Is the hypothesis that the Passion narrative grew like a plant to its present, final stature better founded than that of its being a kind of patchwork quilt? I wonder. Rudolf Bultmann's only argument is that, since Matthew and Luke added some anecdotes to the Markan narrative, it becomes likely that the author of the latter did the same to a previous, shorter form of the Passion story, which in its turn was an expansion of an even earlier one.[95] Matthew's additions that count are the stories of Judas' suicide (27.3–10) and of the guard at the tomb (27.62–66); Luke's are the episodes of the trial before Herod (23.6–16) and of the women of Jerusalem (23.27–31). I said earlier why the Lukan narrative, which also leaves out several of the features of the Markan story, cannot be directly related to it, so that it is meaningless to speak in terms of additions and suppressions when one compares them with each other; they are simply two forms of one original tradition that evolved in several directions. Matthew's additions, on the contrary, were actually inserted in the Markan narrative, but they are unimportant, both in length and for the progression of events. It would be hard to claim that they give strong evidence about the earlier growth of the Passion narrative. In any case, the laws of evolution are not identical here, where a writer copies and enlarges slightly a written text, to what they would be in the evolution of oral tradition and in the process of committing an oral tradition to writing. In other words, we have no evidence at all that the Passion narrative grew from a small nucleus as a plant develops out of a seed.

Am I being too sceptical about the idea of growth applied to tradition? Is it not a self-evident metaphor which requires no demonstration? Is it not required by the inner logic of form-criticism? I do not think so. Oral tradition has its laws, but these vary with the type of tradition and with the kind of transmitting agent.[96] The synoptic tradition may to some extent be compared with rabbinic tradition,[97] but does not obey exactly the same rules. The sayings of Jesus are not handed on exactly in the same way as his miracle stories, etc. Is the tradition of a lengthy, complex narrative like the story of the sufferings and death of Jesus a process of growth or one of reduction, as may have been the case for the miracle stories, if we are to judge from a comparison of Mark and Matthew? Or was it perhaps a transmission *ne varietur*, intended to be literal and unchanging, as was the case with some at least of the sayings of the Master, even if some changes occurred on the occasion of their being translated, collected and written down? All I want to say at this point is that we do not know and that there is no reason to prefer the hypothesis of growth to those of reduction or stability. We shall be able to opt only once we reach some conclusions about the *Sitz im Leben* of the archetype of the canonical Passion narratives.

In sum, although I do not want to be assertive at this point about the way the evolution of the Passion narrative went in pre-synoptic tradition, there is no evidence that it was a growth from the seed of the *kerygma* or any other very short enumeration of the main events of Jesus' sufferings and death.

There is another, even more decisive reason why the *kerygma* should not be considered as the original nucleus of the Passion narrative. The only early *quotation* of that summary of Christian preaching, in I Cor. 15.3ff., leaves no doubt that the Resurrection of Christ and the witness to it of the disciples who had seen the risen Lord were part of it and bore a special emphasis as its triumphant conclusion. Even if two lists of appearances of the risen Christ (vv. 5–6a and v. 7) were combined here either by Paul or in earlier tradition,[98] the original *kerygma* included at least two or three christophanies, which considerably reinforced the assertion that 'he was raised on the third day according to the scriptures' (v. 4b) and thus the weight of the Resurrection in the summary of the main points of the Christian message. In the speeches of the book of Acts, the various forms of the *kerygma* found on the lips of Peter and Paul are somewhat edited in order to fit them to the context; but they all mention the Resurrection and all but one (4.10–12) insist that the apostles were witnesses of it (2.32; 3.15; 5.32; 10.40f.; 13.31), that is, saw the risen Lord (see 10.41 and 13.31) and even ate with him (10.41). There again the Resurrection and its attestations take up a lot of room: one third to one half of the whole *kerygma*. If we consider the synoptic announcements of the Passion and Resurrection of the Son of man (Mark 8.31; 9.31; 10.33f. and par.) as slightly edited forms of the *kerygma*,[99] adapted to a context in which the call to humility and self-sacrifice is the keynote (see Mark 8.34f.; 9.1; 9.33–42; 10.35–45; and par.), we shall not be surprised to find out that they all mention the Resurrection of that figure, but leave out the christophanies. These would indeed have weakened the connection between the prophecy of the Passion and the lesson drawn from it by Jesus and aimed by him at the very witnesses of the appearances of the Risen Lord.

There is thus every reason to think that the early Christian *kerygma* was made up of a brief summary of the life, sufferings and death of Jesus (one half to two thirds of the whole), followed by a mention of the Resurrection and of its biblical foundations, as well as by a list of decisive christophanies. If we compare this structure with the Passion narrative of the Markan gospel, we cannot but be struck by the very limited space devoted there to the Resurrection: eight verses out of a total of 127, that is, a little more than 6 per cent. Add to this the fact that the discovery of the empty tomb, in its Markan form, is hardly more than an allusion to the Resurrection of Jesus and a narrative *impasse*. Is it really conceivable that the *kerygma*, as it grew to the size of the Passion narrative, lost its second half, concerning the Resurrection? I do not think so.

But somebody might object that the three other canonical Passion narratives devote much more space to Resurrection stories and christophanies than the Markan one: 20 verses in Matthew (28. 1–20), that is, nearly 12.5 per cent of the whole Passion in that gospel: 53 verses in Luke (24.1–53), that is, nearly 29.5 per cent of the whole Passion; 29 verses in John (20.1–29), that is, approximately 11 per cent if the Johannine Passion narrative is considered as extending from 13.1 to 20.29. Is then the comparison between the *kerygma* and the Markan narrative distorted for some reason? Should we not leave it aside and base the comparison on the other three?

The trouble is that, as I said earlier,[100] the stories of the christophanies found in Matthew, Luke and John differ so much that they cannot derive from any conceivable common source or be based on

episodes told by the other two. All those christophanies are late
legends that were added to the Passion narratives in order to bring
them nearer to the pattern of the *kerygma*, that is, to emphasize the
Resurrection more than it was emphasized in the archetype of the
stories of the sufferings and death of Jesus. This effort to increase the
similarity between the Passion narratives and the *kerygma* is only
natural in churches that wanted a full account of the life of the
Master and approached this task from the angle of a κύριος
christology, as was the case of the circles where Matthew, Luke and
John were written.

But this effort was needed in the last twenty years of the first
century AD precisely because that similarity did not exist earlier, at
least as far as the post-Resurrection stories are concerned. The
Markan Passion narrative was not affected by that process of
assimilation to the *kerygma* and, as a consequence, takes us back
nearer to the original tradition.

In other words, it is most unlikely that the *kerygma* was the seed
from which the Passion narrative grew. That hypothesis must be
rejected outright and cannot even help us to reconstruct the development of this or that aspect of the archetype of the stories of the
sufferings and death of Jesus as we read them in the gospels. It is
barren, in spite of its apparent attractiveness.

9

Towards the original Passion narrative

Having reached the conclusion that none of the main current hypotheses concerning the origin of the Passion narrative holds water, we now have to go back to concrete evidence, that is to the texts. We are confronted with three narratives, those of Mark, Luke and John, which are built on the same pattern and tell the same story throughout, but differ so much from one another that they are certainly independent from one another, while the Matthaean narrative derives from the Markan story. To account for the striking resemblances between independent narratives, I suggested earlier that the three of them go back to the same archetype, which had evolved in three different directions even before the evangelists appeared on the scene, a process that corresponds exactly to what we know about the history of the gospel tradition in general.[101] To take but one instance of the same evolution of the traditions about Jesus, which was caused or at least encouraged by the growing dispersal of the churches after the fall of Jerusalem in AD 70, the case of Q can be mentioned, since Matthew and Luke doubtless made use of two different forms of what had been originally one source or rather one fund of traditions.[102]

As is the case also for Q, a reconstruction of the exact wording of the archetype of the forms found in the gospels is out of the question for the Passion narrative. It was probably written or rather memorized originally in Aramaic, was then translated into Greek in various places and possibly at various stages of its evolution, while at the same time it evolved in ways we have not been able to establish so far. Only here or there, in the case of key sayings or narrative details, can one hope to approach the original wording with the help of the most exacting scholarship: an instance could be the eucharistic

words of Jesus, analysed by Joachim Jeremias,[103] although his conclusions have not met with general approval. But I shall not launch
on that type of research, which would be time-consuming in the
highest degree and would not help us much in the reconstruction of
the whole of the archetype of the Passion narratives.

What we can actually do towards a reconstruction of the original
narrative is to establish the order and the contents of the episodes of
the Passion, by carefully comparing the three independent stories in
Matthew, Luke and John.

In the first place, all the pericopae or sub-sections of pericopae
which are common to those three narratives and placed at approximately the same juncture were no doubt part of the archetype, even
if there is not much verbal agreement between the three versions.
A list of those common pericopae is easy to draw up and rather
revealing. It begins with an account of the events that took place
during the Last Supper of Jesus with his disciples, including the
announcement of the betrayal by one of those taking part in the
meal (Mark 14.17–25; Luke 22.14–23; John 13.1–30). Then Jesus
and his disciples depart towards a garden on the hill to the east of
the river Kidron (Mark 14.26, 32; Luke 22.39–40a; John 18.1),
although the description of the place varies. There Jesus is arrested
by a police force led by Judas (Mark 14.43–52; Luke 22.47–53;
John 18.2–12), after a vain attempt made by one of the disciples to
resist with a sword in his hand. Jesus is transferred to a high-priestly
residence for the night and man-handled there, while Peter, who had
managed to follow him as far as the courtyard of the mansion, denies
three times having anything to do with him (Mark 14.53a, 54, 65–
72; Luke 22.54–65; John 18.13, 15–18, 22f., 25–27). In the early
morning, a meeting of Jewish leaders decides to hand over the
prisoner to the Roman governor (Mark 15.1; Luke 22.66–23.1;
John 18.24, 28), although this meeting is only implied in John's
story (ἄγουσιν οὖν τὸν Ἰησοῦν . . . at the beginning of v. 28 would be
hard to understand were it not assumed by the writer that some
people had just met at Caiaphas' house to deal with the case of
Jesus). At some time during the night or in the small hours of the
morning, the Jewish authorities had questioned Jesus (Mark 14.
61b–64; Luke 22.67–71; John 18.19–21), who had replied firmly.
Pilate then questions Jesus and 'delivers him to be crucified', after
the Barabbas incident (Mark 15.2–15; Luke 23.2–5, 18–25; John
18.29–40; 19.16a). Jesus is taken to the place called the Skull, there

crucified between two thieves, while the soldiers draw lots for his clothes, utters some sayings and dies after a relatively short agony, attended by some women of his following (Mark 15.20b, 22–27, 34–37, 40–41; Luke 23.26a, 33–38, 46, 49; John 19.16b–19, 23–25, 28–30). Joseph of Arimathaea buries Jesus' body (Mark 15.42–47; Luke 23.50–56; John 19.38–42). Mary of Magdala and some other women followers of Jesus find the tomb empty and meet one or two angels there on the Sunday morning (Mark 16.1–8; Luke 24.1–12; John 20.1f., 11–13), the presence of the other women being only alluded to in John 20.2b (οὐκ οἴδαμεν . . .).

That list of pericopae found in all three independent Passion narratives provides the summary of a perfectly continuous and coherent story of the sufferings and death of Jesus, ending with an episode pointing towards the other central theme in early Christian preaching, the Resurrection of Christ. It is also significant that the events that occurred during the Last Supper should be part and parcel of that story. Any attempt at separating that pericope from the rest of the Passion narrative runs against that state of affairs and would have to proffer very strong evidence indeed in order to prevail over it. To my knowledge, no scholar has ever done it yet.[104]

We have thus reached a good starting-point in our quest for the lost archetype of the canonical Passion narratives. But we must go further. I tried in chapters 4 and 5 to detect the origin of Luke's and John's particular material in the Passion narrative, some of it being editorial and the rest coming from various kinds of tradition. Interesting though it is, this distinction does not help us much in our effort to reconstruct the original Passion narrative, since traditional material found only in the Lukan or the Johannine story of the sufferings and death of our Lord comes mostly from other types of tradition. In order to achieve our goal, we must regard every pericope or sub-section of a pericope found in only one of the three independent Passion narratives as a later addition to the archetype, with a few possible exceptions here and there.

The most conspicuous case of this kind of addition is of course the Farewell Discourse in John 13–17. On a smaller scale, we have the Farewell Speech in Luke 22.24–38, which is based to a much larger extent on sayings of the Lord preserved by tradition, but none the less was not part of the original Passion narrative and was added when the pressure of literary convention caused the lack of a moving Farewell Speech on the lips of Jesus to become unbearable.[105] A number of other instances may also be mentioned: in Luke, the questioning of Jesus by Herod (23.6–12), perhaps a creation of the evangelist to illustrate the statement made in Acts 4.27f. as a kind of *midrash pesher* on Ps 2.1f., quoted in Acts 4.25f.; the words addressed by Jesus to the women of Jerusalem in Luke 23.27–31; the dialogue with the penitent thief in Luke 23.30–43; in the Fourth Gospel, the scene with the mother of Jesus and the Beloved Disciple (19.25–27); the blow with the spear (19.31–36); etc. All the appearances of the risen Christ in Luke and John should be added, since they have nothing in common, as we noted earlier, and of course have no counterpart in Mark. In sum, there is no pericope or sub-section of a pericope found exclusively in the Lukan or the Johannine Passion narrative that could be considered as part of the original Passion story.

Things are not quite as clear in the case of the features of the Markan narrative which have no counterpart in Luke and John. Since there is little editorial material in Mark 14–16,[106] those features stand a reasonable chance of belonging to the archetype and having been left aside by Luke and John for literary or theological motives every time such motives can be detected. Mark 14.9 has no parallel in Luke because the whole story of the anointing in Bethany was cut out in that gospel for literary reasons; it has no counterpart in John because the idea of commemorating in a special way the action of a human being is not acceptable to the evangelist who insists that the disciples should remember the words and deeds *of their Master* (John 2.22; 14.26; 15.20; 16.4); it may therefore come from the archetype or at least from an early form of the Markan story. Mark 14.28 seems to be an editorial note added by the writer who brought together Mark 1–13 and Mark 14–16,[107] but Mark 14.27 is a different matter, because it is an excellent introduction to vv. 29–31, which certainly belonged to the archetype (although perhaps not with that wording); besides, it has an acceptable parallel in John 16.32 and even Luke makes an allusion to the flight of the disciples in 22.32b; we should count it as part of the original Passion story.

On the contrary, there is no reason why Mark 14.33f. should be part of the archetype of the Passion narratives; it arose, like other features of the Markan story of the prayer at Gethsemane, through a midrashic development of the original narration that connected it with Pss. 42–43.[108] The same remark applies to Mark 14.38b–42, that is, to the last verses of that story. The incident of the flight of the naked young man at the time of the arrest of Jesus (Mark 14. 51f.) may well have belonged to the original Passion narrative and have been suppressed by Luke and John because it detracted in their eyes from the dramatic solemnity of the narrative. As for the episode of the false witnesses during the trial of Jesus before the high priest (Mark 14.55–61a), it probably vanished in Luke when this evangelist decided to do away with the night session of the Sanhedrin, and in John because the latter wanted to rewrite the same episode in order to bring it down to the size of a mere unofficial questioning;[109] both moves resulted from apologetic motives, as also did the changes made by Matthew in the Markan text at this point;[110] the narrative as it stood in the archetype had no doubt been criticized for its improbability; it was doubtless very similar to Mark 14.55–61a.

Mark 15.10f. is, it seems, an editorial expansion of the Barabbas episode, but the possibility that these verses came from the archetype cannot be entirely ruled out; their absence in the Lukan and Johannine parallels might then be explained by a tendency in tradition to do away with useless details in lengthy narratives. Mark 15.25 was suppressed by Matthew as pointless; Luke and John offer no parallel because they found the time-table of the crucifixion which we read in Mark rather preposterous;[111] although one can agree with them to a certain extent, one has to acknowledge the fact that, being a kind of *lectio difficilior*, Mark 15.25 must have been part of the original Passion narrative. The mocking of Jesus on the cross by the passers-by (Mark 15.29f.) has no parallel in John, because that gospel suppressed all mention of mockeries in the crucifixion story; although Luke tried to show the attitude of the crowd to have been more sympathetic to Jesus (see Luke 23.48), there is no doubt that he had some knowledge of less friendly behaviour on the part of the Jewish masses and felt he could do no more than describe it as neutral (Luke 23.35a); thus, Mark 15.29f. corresponds to some element of the original Passion narrative. The same is true of Mark 15.34f., 36b, since v. 36a, which is closely linked with it, has parallels both in Luke 23.36 and in John 19.29, while the suppression of the Hebrew quotation from Ps. 22.2 and of the two references to Elijah that go with it is only to be expected, for literary reasons in Luke, where foreign words are usually banned, and for theological motives in both Luke and John, where a cry of despair on the part of Jesus would be unbearable. Mark 15.44f. could be a legendary expansion of an originally brief story, but it could equally well be part of the archetype of the Passion narratives, later left out by Luke and John or by the tradition they made use of; if the latter is the case, a number of motives could be mentioned in order to account for the shortening of the episode: a wish to avoid useless details, a desire to interpret the centurion's words at the foot of the cross as a confession of faith and not simply as an amazed cry at the quick deliverance granted to Jesus in his agony (cf. Mark 15.39 and 15.44f.), etc.

If we leave aside those few verses of Mark that lack parallels, but may come from the original Passion narrative for various reasons, it is clear that pericopae or subsections of them which exist in one of the three independent stories only did not belong to the archetype of the canonical Passion narratives. The problem that remains open is that of the pericopae or subsections of pericopae which are found in two of the three independent stories of the sufferings and death of Jesus. My contention is that most of them were part of the original narrative and that we can easily detect the reasons why the third evangelist or the tradition he made use of did away with such episodes, or at least displaced them.

Things are especially clear in the case of the plot against Jesus, with which the Passion narratives of Mark and Luke begin (Mark 14.1f.; Luke 22.1f.); as we noted earlier,[112] John brought that episode forward in order to link it to the story of the resurrection of Lazarus; we can take it for granted that the archetype of the gospel narratives opened with some remarks about the decision reached shortly before Passover by the Jewish authorities in Jerusalem to have Jesus killed surreptitiously for fear of popular disturbances.

The story of the anointing in Bethany (Mark 14.3–9) has a close parallel in John 12.1–8, which the Fourth Evangelist also brought forward for the reason just mentioned.[113] Its suppression in Luke is due to a literary cause: the choice made by that evangelist of the story of the anointing in the Pharisee's house (Luke 7.36–50), which he considered as a better version of the same story.[114] The anointing in Bethany was part of the original narrative, as the first of the two acted prophecies that associated the followers of Jesus with the death he was about to suffer alone.[115]

The betrayal by Judas (Mark 14.10f.) is paralleled in Luke 22.3–6, but not in John. There is however no doubt that the Fourth Evangelist knew that event, since it is alluded to in 6.71, 12.4 and 13.2 and announced as imminent in 13.27b and 13.30. It was part of the original narrative.

The preparation for the Passover meal is told by Mark (14.12–17) and Luke (22.7–14) in closely parallel narratives. John did away with it because it was not compatible with his identification of Jesus with the paschal lamb (see John 19.31–33, 35f.), a theory which made it necessary to remove any paschal feature attached to the last meal in Christian tradition,[116] that is, in fact, the episode of the preparation. That episode was thus part of the archetype of the Passion narratives.

The institution of the Lord's Supper is common to Mark and Luke, in spite of important divergences between them (Mark 14.22–25; Luke 22.15–20). It is lacking in John, not, as has sometimes been claimed,[117] because there was an anti-sacramental strain in that gospel, but because it clashed with the evangelist's idea of the eucharistic bread *being* the Body of Christ (John 6.51–58) after the end of the earthly life of Jesus, in a sense which cannot be identical with that of the words 'This is my body' uttered by the living Master. Having been suppressed by the fourth evangelist, this episode belonged to the original Passion narrative.

The announcement of Peter's denial on the way to the Mount of Olives, as recorded in Mark 14.29–31, has no full parallel in Luke and John, where that episode is located in the upper room and belongs to the Farewell Discourse (Luke 22.31–34; John 13.36–38). This discourse being an editorial feature of those two gospels, the context suggested by Mark may be the original one. In any case, the prophecy of Peter's denial goes back to the archetype of the Passion narratives.

In spite of all differences between them, the versions of the prayer at Gethsemane found in Mark 14.32–42 and Luke 22.39–46 point towards the same episode. John inserted the core of that story, that is, Jesus' anguish and his prayer of submission to the Father's will, in the midst of the anecdote of the Greeks who asked to see the Master (12.23–28; see in particular v. 27). The rest of it was in bad taste in the eyes of an evangelist who constantly insisted on Jesus' mastery over the events and over himself; he therefore cut it out. My conclusion is that the prayer at Gethsemane belonged to the original Passion narrative in a form resembling the part of the story which Mark and Luke have in common.

The episode of the mocking of Jesus by the Roman soldiers (Mark 15.16–20a) has its counterpart in John 19.2f., that is, in the midst of the Roman trial instead of following the verdict as in Mark. But

Luke left it out, or rather replaced it by a brief notice on the way the soldiers took their share in mocking Jesus on the cross (Luke 23.36f.). The apologetic intention of this editorial reduction of a theme that was fairly important in Mark and John cannot be denied. We thus have every reason to think that the archetype of the Passion narratives associated a scene of mocking by the soldiers with the Roman trial of Jesus.

Mark 15.21 and Luke 23.26 mention the drafting of Simon of Cyrene to carry Jesus' cross. John makes no allusion to that incident, but apparently wants to reject the idea that Jesus did not carry his cross himself, since 19.17a asserts that he did. The Fourth Gospel has no use for an episode which suggests that the Master was exhausted and had to be helped. There is every chance that its tradition of the Passion narrative included this incident. In other words, Simon of Cyrene was mentioned in the three stories of the Passion, a sure sign that he had a part in the earliest narrative of the sufferings and death of our Lord.

The mocking of Jesus on the cross (Mark 15.28–32 and Luke 23.35–37) has no counterpart in John, who doubtless felt this episode detracted from the dignity of the dramatic scene of the crucifixion and from Jesus' mastery over all the events of the Passion. It was part of the archetype of the Passion narratives, probably with two subsections as in Mark, since the Lukan form seems to have been edited.[118]

In sum, there is every reason to consider the episodes of the Passion which are reported in two of the independent narratives only as parts of the original story of the sufferings and death of Jesus. We cannot be absolutely sure of the contents of those episodes in their earliest form, but their presence is a certainty.

Having examined the likelihood of that presence in the case of pericopae found both once only and three times, we are now in a position to sum up our findings and draw a list of all the elements included in the original Passion narrative:

1. The plot against Jesus shortly before Passover.
2. The anointing in Bethany, the first acted prophecy of Jesus' death.
3. The betrayal by Judas.
4. The preparation for the Passover meal.
5. The events that took place during that meal, recorded in an

unknown order: announcement of the betrayal, eating and drinking by the disciples as a second acted prophecy of the death of Jesus, some sayings of Jesus.

6. The announcement of Peter's denial, probably on the way to Gethsemane.

7. The prayer in Gethsemane, in a form including a mention of Jesus' anguish and of the disciples' sleep, but much simpler than the Markan version.

8. The arrest of Jesus by a police force led by Judas, with a short note about an attempt at forcible resistance by one of the followers of the Master, a saying of Jesus, a brief remark on the flight of the disciples and probably the anecdote concerning the naked young man.

9. The trial before the Sanhedrin, including the episode of the false witnesses and some mention of the man-handling of Jesus.

10. Peter's denial of his Master in the high priest's courtyard on three successive occasions.

11. New meeting of the Sanhedrin in the early morning and delivery of Jesus to Pilate.

12. The Roman trial of Jesus, including a fairly full form of the Barabbas episode and ending with the remark that Pilate 'delivered him to be crucified'.

13. The mocking of Jesus by the Roman soldiers.

14. The drafting of Simon of Cyrene to carry Jesus' cross to Golgotha.

15. The crucifixion between two thieves, the sharing of Jesus' clothes between the soldiers, the *titulus* with the phrase 'King of the Jews', the time-table as in Mark, the mocking by the crowds, by the Jewish leaders and by the crucified thieves, the three hours of darkness at midday, Jesus' Hebraic prayer to God and reactions to it, Jesus' death, the rending of the temple veil and the centurion's remark.

16. The women watching from a distance.

17. The burial of Jesus by Joseph of Arimathaea, including perhaps Pilate's inquiry about the death.

18. The discovery of the empty tomb by some women, led by Mary of Magdala, who receive a message from an angel.

As I said earlier, this is merely a list of narrative elements, some long and some short, and leaves open the question of the wording of each of the episodes mentioned, because we have no means of reconstructing a word by word text of the archetype of the Passion narratives. In spite of that serious limitation of our enterprise, I note that this skeleton of a narrative is closely akin to the outline of the Markan narrative in chs. 14–16. In other words, the Passion according to Mark may have developed some of the pericopae in the original story (e.g. no. 7 above), or reduced some (e.g. no. 11), but it did not alter its outline and, even if its wording evolved considerably, it was not edited in any systematic way.[119]

A Sitz im Leben *for the original Passion narrative*

Thanks to a detailed analysis of the four canonical Passion narratives, we have been able so far to reconstruct the skeleton of the earliest form of the story of the sufferings and death of Jesus and to show that this original Passion narrative, a continuous and coherent literary piece from its inception, was neither a mere record of facts, nor a *midrash* on some Old Testament texts, nor an expanded form of the *kerygma* of the early church. But what exactly was this rather large tradition unit, which a small and poor religious group would not have been able to memorize and hand down so successfully for a generation or two if it had not served a practical purpose in its life? In other words, what was the *Sitz im Leben* of the earliest Passion narrative?

Some of the features of our canonical stories of the sufferings and death of Jesus will help us in that difficult quest, which no comparison with other tradition units of the early church can alleviate, since the rest of synoptic tradition is made up of short, unconnected stories and collections of sayings.

In the first place, it is striking that the story of the arrest, the trial and the execution of a religious leader like Jesus should begin with the anointing in Bethany, a strange gesture which the Master interprets even more strangely, soon followed by the story of the Last Supper, characterized by the queer selection of sayings and events made by the narrator. Many other events that had taken place just before Jesus' arrest – or that were supposed to have taken place then – might have been reported and would have been more to the point, at least at first glance: for instance, Jesus' farewell remarks or discourse to his disciples, as in the case of the dying Socrates and in so many 'testaments' left by great Israelites of the past to their heirs, according to Jewish writers of that period;[120] or the last miracles wrought by Jesus, a feature conspicuously absent from the Passion narratives apart from Luke's hurried allusion to the healing of the ear of the high priest's servant (22.51b), whereas it would have stressed most convincingly what powers Jesus had refused to use in order to submit to the will of God. But as a matter of fact, the anointing in Bethany and the Last Supper were chosen by the narrator. I described those two episodes as acted prophecies of the death of Jesus and as occasions offered to the followers of the Master to be associated with that death. Is it not significant also that this association takes the form of gestures that can only be described as cultic: the wasteful anointing of the Lord one worships; the eating and drinking of sacred food? Of course, we do not know what cultic context is presupposed by those actions, although the story of the Last Supper was told in relation with the celebration of the Eucharist (see I Cor. 11.23–26). But some cultic practice might have associated the two episodes, since these are closely linked in the Passion narrative. I shall come back to that.

The episode of the preparation of the Passover meal implies some liturgical actions of two disciples, who take the usual dispositions for the eating of 'the Pascha' (Mark 14.12 and par.), i.e. doubtless the paschal lamb of the traditional Jewish Passover celebration,[121] by Jesus and his followers. This scene may be purely legendary or have an historical basis – it does not matter at this juncture. What makes it important from the angle of my quest of a *Sitz im Leben* for the earliest Passion narrative is that it links the eucharistic words uttered by the Master during the meal and the actions he orders his disciples to perform with the Jewish Passover meal, its calendar and its rites. Whatever one thinks of that connexion, the episode of the preparation of the Last Supper thus contributes greatly to reinforce the liturgical colouring of the beginning of the archetype of the Passion narratives.

Another feature of the earliest Passion narrative which may be noted here is its chronological framework. I said earlier how unlikely it is from the historian's point of view, because it crams too many events into much too short a time.[122] If one accepts that conclusion, one then has to account for the choice of such a tight schedule by the original narrator. After the Passover meal, which takes place soon after sunset, less than twenty-four hours elapse till the burial of Jesus. No detailed time-table is suggested for the events of the night extending from the beginning of the Last Supper to just before the early morning meeting of the Sanhedrin. But some features of the narrative give a kind of rhythm to the main events: the division of the prayer in Gethsemane into three episodes, even if it is a some-what later development of the Markan tradition suggested by the structure of Pss. 42 and 43,[123] gives it, by its repetitiveness, the appearance of an incantation or a sacred dance; the triple denial of Jesus by Peter, which is part of the original narrative, is also very repetitive and adds an element of dramatic tension to the Jewish trial, while it also contributes some chronological notes (see Mark 14.72 and par.; Luke 22.58f.). Could the repetitiveness and the ternary structure of those two episodes have something to do with their *Sitz im Leben,* either at birth or later in tradition? It might indeed be suggested that the first of them appeared in a liturgical setting (prayer of submission to God's will) and was further used in worship in its Markan form, while the latter derived its striking ternary pattern from some kind of cultic drama in which it was embedded from the start.

The time-table becomes much more precise from dawn on: Jesus is handed over to Pilate by the Sanhedrin πρωΐ, that is before sun-rise, according to Mark 15.1 and John 18.28, or early in the morn-ing, according to Luke 22.66 and 23.1; he is crucified at the third hour, i.e. at 9 a.m., according to Mark 15.25; darkness engulfs the whole earth from 12 noon to 3 p.m., according to Mark 15.33 and Luke 23.44–45a; at the ninth hour, that is, at 3 p.m., Jesus utters his last words and soon dies (Mark 15.34–37); ὀψίας γενομένης, that is, shortly before or after sunset, around 6 p.m., Joseph of Arimathaea sees to Jesus' burial (Mark 15.42; cf. Luke 23.54). What is very striking about this time-table is the way in which it records events every three hours, from 6 a.m. to 6 p.m. It has been noted that those times of day coincided with the hours of prayer of the Jews.[124] Is there a connexion? Is it a coincidence that the least edited of the canonical Passion narratives, Mark 14–16, should provide the most complete form of that strange schedule? The answer is, I believe, that the time-table was part of the original story and was progressively eliminated when its meaning was not perceived any longer, that is, when the Passion narrative became a mere record of events. In other words, the archetype of the Passion narratives was something different which took into consideration some features of Jewish worship. It seems only natural to assume that a tradition of this kind had its *Sitz im Leben* in the worshipping life of a Christian community which was still influenced by Jewish customs.

Finally, it is significant also that the last two episodes in the original Passion narrative should have to do with the paying of the last honours to the body of Jesus according to the rites of the Jews (Mark 15.46 and par.; Mark 16.1f. and par.). The narrator might have chosen to conclude the story of the sufferings and death of the Master in various other ways: a description of the spectacular consequences of Jesus' death for the *kosmos* (see Matt. 27.51–54); a description of the Resurrection itself (see Gospel according to Peter, 35–44); some christophanies (as in Matthew, Luke and John); etc. By his choice of the episodes of the burial and of the empty tomb, he put the emphasis on the liturgical element, just as he had done at the beginning of the Passion narrative by selecting the stories of the anointing in Bethany and of the Last Supper.

A number of features of the original Passion narrative thus point towards a liturgical setting for this tradition unit. It might of course be objected that the style of the Passion narratives as we read them in the canonical gospels does not bear the mark of liturgical solemnity, characterized by the rhythmical prose of Phil. 2.5–11, of some hymns of the book of Revelation (e.g. chs. 4–5) and of the prologue of the Fourth Gospel, or by the long-winded sentences of some confession-like pieces in the Pauline epistles (e.g. Col. 1.9–23; Eph. 1.3–23; etc.) and of some of the discourses of Jesus in the Fourth Gospel (e.g. 5.19–47; 6.26–58; etc.). The story of the sufferings and death of the Master, if one leaves aside the Farewell Speeches in John 13–17, is indeed written in a style that is neither rhythmical, nor wordy.

But does that mean that it cannot have liturgical roots? If we are to judge from the Lord's Prayer, which is doubtless the oldest liturgical piece of some size that came down to us from the early church,[125] prolixity was not encouraged in the earliest Christian liturgies (see Matt. 6.7–13). If we look at the synoptic tradition, we certainly do not gain the impression that the production of confessions of the faith and of hymns was a major part in the worshipping life of early Palestinian Christians, to the extent that this would have established a pattern of liturgical style.[126] It is therefore impossible to use stylistic criteria to refute the hypothesis of a liturgical origin of the Passion narrative, the original wording of which we do not even know.

But some comparisons with the liturgy of Jewish festivals will help us to verify the likelihood of that conjecture. Although the meaning of Pentecost was not historicized as early as that of the Passover, it became in the eyes of the rabbis, from the second century AD on, the celebration of the revelation of the Torah to Moses on Mount Sinai as was suggested by the chronological note in Exod. 19.1. It is furthermore likely that Pentecost had acquired that meaning a good deal earlier in some Jewish circles.[127] The liturgy of that festival in the synagogues doubtless included the reading of Exod. 19ff., the story of the event which was commemorated that day.

We stand on firmer ground about the feast of Purim, which among Jews was the commemoration of the salvation of their people from the slaughter ordered by Haman, Prime Minister of King Ahasuerus of Persia (486–465 BC). The book of Esther, which told the story of those dramatic events, was read in all the synagogues on the day of Purim, as the central part of the liturgy.[128]

As for Passover, which quite early became the commemoration of Israel's exodus from Egypt, it was celebrated to a large extent in the homes, where the Passover Eve supper was held according to a liturgy, the *seder*, in which a *haggadah* of the Exodus story played a major part. This *haggadah* varied considerably at the time of Jesus and of the beginnings of Christianity, in order to satisfy the needs of the groups taking part in the celebration.[129] It always referred to the story of the exodus as it was told in the Pentateuch, and more specifically in the book of Exodus. It is most likely that some excerpts of that book were read.

In sum, the liturgy of at least three of the Jewish festivals included at the beginning of the Christian era the reading of a lengthy narrative telling the story of the events that were celebrated on those days, or at least a kind of *midrash* on that story. This is an enlightening parallel, which makes it even more likely that the archetype of the Passion narratives had its roots in some liturgy.

In view of all the features of the Passion narratives which have a liturgical ring about them and of this parallel, it is my contention that Archbishop Philip Carrington was right when, in his otherwise largely fanciful book on *The Primitive Christian Calendar*,[130] he suggested that the Markan Passion story originated as the *megillah*, the scroll, to be read at an early Christian celebration of the sufferings and death of Christ held on the occasion of the Jewish Passover. If we are cautious enough to separate this illuminating conjecture from the wider theory Carrington develops in his book as to the whole of the Markan gospel, as well as from the details he goes into about it, no serious objection can be raised against that idea.

Of course, very little is known about the attitude of the first Christian generation towards yearly festivals. We have a little more evidence about the Sabbath and Sunday celebrations, but even on that point much remains in the dark.[131] Paul's extreme views on those matters (see Gal. 4.8–11; Col. 2.16–23), mitigated only for pastoral reasons (see Rom. 14.1–6), did not prevail in most parts of the early church, where the Jewish calendar was still in use as far as we can see.[132] There can be little doubt that among Jewish Christians Jewish festivals were celebrated and, in some cases at least, were the occasion for a pilgrimage to the Jerusalem temple (see Acts 20.16; 21.26; 24.11). It seems only natural that on the day of the Passover, which was also the anniversary of the death of Jesus, Christians should have wanted to commemorate not only the Exodus, but also the sufferings and death of their Lord, whose execution and triumph over death had freed them from the bondage of sin.

The *Sitz im Leben* of the original Passion narrative thus was doubtless the liturgical commemoration of Christ's death by Christians during the Jewish Passover celebration.

The original Passion narrative in its historical context

Although the Jewish Passover celebration was already in the first century AD a family affair that took place in every home according to a ritual that is reasonably well known to us,[133] the pull of the Jerusalem temple, as the one place of worship for Israel, was felt by all the Jews on that occasion. Thousands of people flocked to the Holy City as pilgrims, filled whatever accommodation was available there, camped in the valleys and on the hills outside the city walls, in order to be able to slaughter their lamb in the temple and to hold their Passover Eve meal wherever they could inside Jerusalem.[134] The Passover pilgrimage was the largest in the year. There can be no doubt that among the pilgrims thus gathered for a few days in the capital some were Jews who had recognized Jesus as the Messiah, at least during the thirty-odd years preceding the beginning of the Jewish War in AD 66.

Those Christian pilgrims from Palestine and beyond came to a city where they had brethren. In spite of all the obscurities that remain about the events following the death of Jesus, it is certain that a large Christian congregation existed in Jerusalem at a very early date after the crucifixion. These people may have gathered in the capital partly because they expected the *parousia* of the Lord to take place there, an attitude which some other Christians objected to as a vain attempt at localizing that eschatological advent (Mark 13.21–27 and par.; Luke 17.20–37). But another reason for the Jerusalem Christians to reside there surely was their desire to worship in the temple, even if they did not approve of the animal sacrifices that the priests considered as their special duty under the

law of Moses.[135] The information offered on that point in the book
of Acts, scanty though it may be, leaves no doubt that they went
there to pray quite frequently (see Acts 2.46; 3.1; 5.12f., 21, 42).
They took advantage of the crowd gathered in the temple courts and
porticoes to preach the gospel whenever they had a chance and were
not prevented from doing so by the temple police. They were thus
bound to make a special effort every time large crowds of pilgrims
assembled there, that is especially for the main festivals of the year
and first of all on the occasion of Passover.

Passover was a day when Jerusalem Christians and Jewish Christian pilgrims both went to the temple in large numbers and inevitably
met there. But they would also have specific reasons to get together
on that day. To both groups, this was the moving anniversary of the
crucifixion, which had taken place in Jerusalem some years earlier
and some commemoration of that tragic event was only natural. In
addition, the Jerusalem church was in the eyes of all Christians till
the Jewish War not only the oldest and probably the largest of all
congregations of the faithful, but also the main seat of authority and
the chief fount of tradition, owing to the presence in its midst of the
Twelve and of James, brother of the Lord (see Acts, *passim* and
Gal. 1.15–2.10; Rom. 15.25–28; etc.). In spite of all the tensions
and problems that arose among Christians in those days, as illustrated for instance in Paul's epistle to the Galatians, it would have
been unthinkable for a Jewish Christian pilgrim to the Jerusalem
temple to stay away from the mother church: Paul's behaviour in
Acts 21.17–26 is no doubt typical in that regard, even if the narrative
is somewhat biased.[136]

In other words, the Jerusalem congregation and the Christian
pilgrims got together every time a pilgrimage took place during
those thirty-odd years, particularly on the occasion of the Passover.
There can be no doubt that, in addition to the commemoration of
the exodus, they felt impelled to celebrate the anniversary of their
Master's death on the cross. Was there a better way to do that than
by listening together to the story of the Passion, ending with the
episode of the empty tomb, which was the perfect allusion to the
mystery of Christ's Resurrection, heart of their common faith? My
contention therefore is that the archetype of the Passion narratives
was the story that was told on those occasions, perhaps three or four
times a year, but mostly on the day of Passover.

Is it possible to be more specific about the liturgy of those celebrations? It seems almost certain that some of the Old Testament texts alluded to or quoted in the Passion narrative were read, perhaps also commented upon: Pss. 22 and 69; Isa. 52.13–53.12, etc. Some prayers were no doubt said, some hymns sung, but we do not know what they were. It can also be assumed that a moving ceremony of this kind made room for some active participation of those attending it, who may have been invited to meet and adjourn at the same rhythm as the story itself, to go from one place to another as the narrative suggested, to make worshipping gestures as some episodes were read, to take part in a special Eucharist while they listened to the story of the Last Supper. All these suggestions remain purely hypothetical, although there is nothing intrinsically improbable about any of them. They do not allow a reconstruction of the liturgy of the Christian Passover celebration in Jerusalem.

Some scholars object to that cautious conclusion and try their hand at reconstructing in some detail the liturgical background of the Passion narrative. For instance, Gottfried Schille conjectured three cultic poles around which the narrative had found its present structure:[137] an *anamnesis* of the last night of Jesus' life, ending with the cock-crow and attached, it seems, to an *agape* lasting the whole night (Mark 14.18–72 and par.); a celebration of Good Friday linked with the hours of prayer usual among Jews (Mark 15.2–41); an Easter morning liturgy, possibly held near the site of Jesus' tomb (Mark 15.42–16.8). The evidence for this reconstruction is slender, even though it is fairly attractive in parts. It is enough to say that the Passover celebrations which gave birth to the Passion narrative may not have been held at one spot only and as a continuous performance; it was perhaps divided into two or three parts held at different times of day and possibly at two or three different places in and around Jerusalem. In any case, it was a solemn liturgy that brought together the Jerusalem church and the pilgrims who acknowledged Jesus as the Messiah.

The chronology of the beginnings of the Jerusalem church and of Christian missions is too vague for us to say when that celebration was first held. But, if one assumes that Jesus died in AD 30 and that his disciples did not stay away from the capital for more than a few months or at most a few years,[138] it is a conservative estimate to suggest that the Christian Passover liturgy and its *megillah* were in existence before AD 40 – less than ten years after the events they commemorated. Several features of the Markan narrative, which I said is the least edited of the canonical Passion stories, confirm the likelihood of an early dating of the original narrative. Some obscure people are mentioned there, as though they were bound to be known to the hearers of that story: the naked young man (14.51f.); Alexander and Rufus, the sons of the man who bore Jesus' cross to Golgotha (15.21); Salome, one of the women who followed Jesus (15.40 and 16.1). None of them is mentioned in the other gospels or known from the rest of the New Testament, as the Rufus of Romans 16.13 is unlikely to be the same person as that of Mark 15.21. Having witnessed this or that episode of the Passion, they were still familiar figures among Jerusalem Christians ten years later. Twenty to forty years after the redaction of the Passion narrative, they were left out of tradition as it had evolved, because they had become totally unknown quantities for all Christians.

If an early date is accepted for the formation of the narrative linked with the Jerusalem celebration of the Passion, ought we to have second thoughts about the historical reliability of this story?[139] I do not think so. Of course, the general likelihood of the facts recorded is reinforced, since witnesses of the events were present among the listeners and had fairly fresh memories. But that is all. The place names mentioned in the narrative certainly correspond to localities that were well known in and around Jerusalem in those days. Unfortunately, Jerusalem was twice razed to the ground (AD 70 and 135) and deprived of all its population before being rebuilt as a Roman city, while the Christian church there first had to go into exile and then was replaced by a totally different congregation with no Jewish roots.[140] Besides, it is only in the fourth century that Christians began to take an interest in the places where Jesus had suffered and died, under the pressure of a new generation of pilgrims, who wanted to worship on the very spots where Christ had been. In other words, there is no continuity whatever between the concrete localizations of the years 30–70 and the arbitrary designations attempted three hundred years later. This or that identification may have been correct, but we are no longer able to prove that it corresponds to what the narrator of the Passion story had in mind.

The situation is somewhat similar for the chronology of the narrative, except that, as I said earlier,[141] it was moulded by liturgical influences and thus less likely to be historical than the topography. In this case, too, there is a wide gap between the Jerusalem of AD 30–70 and the Roman city which took its place. With the discovery of the Qumran Scrolls, modern scholars rediscovered the violent quarrels that tore apart the Jewish people of those days as to the choice of a calendar and the impact those questions may have had on the chronology of the Passion.[142] I cannot go into this here. The outcome of the discussion of the additional information thus acquired is that a reconstruction of the chronology of the events of the Passion may take us even farther away from the Passion narrative than was imagined earlier.

The early date of the original Passion narrative is no guarantee either that it reflects correctly the legal situation in Jerusalem at the time. The difficulties I noted earlier[143] are far from negligible and show how ignorant first-generation Christians were on matters of law and the judicial system. There is nothing surprising in that ignorance, which is due both to the nature of the Passion narrative and to the cultural shortcomings of those plain people.

This being said, the archetype of the Passion narratives had its roots so close to the events of the sufferings and death of Jesus, chronologically, topographically and spiritually speaking, that it cannot be totally fanciful. I must stress at this point, even more emphatically than I did earlier,[144] that the main features of the story and of the political and religious background it presupposes are historically sound. As a matter of fact, the earliest Passion narrative is a first-class document about the life and the daily working of major institutions like the temple, the Sanhedrin, the Roman governor, in the Jerusalem of the first half of the first century AD, provided it is not used uncritically.

It is also a most interesting document about the life and thought of the early Jerusalem church. Even though it does not give us any information about the organization and the daily and weekly gatherings of the congregation, it implicitly confirms what the first chapters of the book of Acts say about the part played by the Twelve (see Mark 14.17ff. and par.), by Peter, James and John (see Mark 14.33ff. and the Matthaean parallel) and especially by Peter, who is frequently mentioned in the narrative. The Passion story also suggests that Jerusalem Christians kept the daily hours of prayer usual among Jews (see the crucifixion in Mark 15.25, 33f.), as well as the sabbath (see Mark 15.42–16.2 and par.), two features that Acts take for granted. The Passion narrative is more explicit about other, less frequent celebrations held in the Jerusalem church: the commemorations of Jesus' sufferings and death on the main Jewish festivals, specially on the day of the Passover; the part played by the Lord's Supper in that liturgy; the use of aromatic spices at the beginning and at the end of that solemn service (cf. the anointing in Bethany and the women at the tomb, Mark 14.3–9; 16.1ff. and par.); the call to prayer launched to the congregation taking part in that ceremony (cf. the prayer in Gethsemane and the crucifixion narrative); and finally the emotional tone of the whole commemoration as emphasized by the themes of plot, betrayal, inability of the disciples to follow their Master to the end, bad faith and brutality on the part of Jesus' enemies, serene acceptance of the will of God by Jesus.

The Passion narrative also gives us some insights as to the thought of the early Jerusalem church, particularly in the field of christology. The many allusions to scripture all through the story show that every detail in the sufferings and death of our Lord was related to some prophecy, which it was supposed to have fulfilled. Apart from what this fact suggests as to the authority of the Old Testament in the eyes of the Christians in Jerusalem,[145] it also leaves no doubt that much of the christology of that earliest of churches is derived from scripture: Jesus is neither the destroyer of the temple (Mark 14.57–59 and par.), the blasphemer (Mark 14.63f. and par.) and the rebel (Mark 15.2ff. and par.) he was accused of being, nor simply the teacher he also was (Mark 14.14, 49 and par.), but the mysterious founder of a New Covenant by the shedding of his blood (Mark 14.24 and par.), the new David who joins in the prayer of Ps. 41 and foresees a glorious future for himself beyond betrayal and suffering (Mark 14.18–21 and par.), the Shepherd of Israel whose death is the apparent end of the people of God according to Zech. 13.7ff. (Mark 14.27 and par.), the Christ, the Son of God and the Son of man of Dan. 7.13 and Ps. 110.1 (Mark 14.61f. and par.; 15.39 and par.), the King of the Jews (Mark 15.2 and par.; etc. . . .) and, on the cross, the Servant of Ps. 22 and Isa. 53 (Mark 15.22–39 and par.). This profusion of christological titles and names comes as a confirmation of the scattered and unsystematic christology expressed in the synoptic tradition and in the speeches of Acts 1–13, that is, of the efforts of the early Jerusalem church to try and account for the life, the death and the resurrection of Jesus.[146] Faced with that unregulated but high christology, Gentile Christians and second- and third-generation Jewish Christians had to build their own doctrine of Christ through a process of selection and organization, rather than one of creation.[147]

In sum, the Passion narrative could be described as the best reflection of the face of the early Church, that bunch of plain, pious, brave and somewhat shy Palestinian Jews who found themselves in charge of a shattering message, were not too sure how to go about spreading it, and tended to lose themselves in the contemplation of God's mighty acts. It took the brutality of the 'Hellenists' and the wide perspectives of Paul to turn the eyes of Christians towards the outside world and to liberate the gospel from its Jerusalem fetters. We may be grateful that this was achieved without the loss of the Jerusalem heritage, particularly as regards that irreplaceable master-piece, the Passion narrative.

CONCLUSION

At the end of the fairly arduous road which I tried to open through the canonical Passion narratives, some readers may perhaps wonder whether it was worth the trouble. Are we any wiser in our understanding of the sufferings and death of our Lord? Can we really read those narratives better than we did before? Has it become easier for us to explain to the men of to-day what the cross means in their life?

No extravagant claim would be in order at this point. I cannot pretend to have solved all the literary problems of the four Passion narratives. It has not been possible to reconstruct the text of the original Passion story and I have had to admit that the liturgy in which it was used could not be brought back to light in any detail. The last days of Jesus' life remain shrouded in darkness and none of the well-known historical problems connected with them is nearer a final solution. As to the theology, and particularly the christology, underlying the narratives, no clear picture arises at the end of this investigation, since the Jerusalem church does not seem to have attempted a synthesis of the various christological themes recorded in its traditions, including the Passion narrative.

This being said, the results reached are to my mind a considerable help for the reading and interpretation of the Passion narratives of the canonical gospels. Since the original form of those narratives was a liturgical text used as the basis of a solemn commemoration of the sufferings and death of Jesus by the Jerusalem church within a few years of the actual events, it becomes easier to ask the right questions, from the angles of history, theology and literary criticism. Thus, as I tried to show in this study, we stand a much better chance of finding satisfactory answers without having to squeeze and twist the texts.

But the queries of the sceptical readers cannot be totally dismissed unless we go one step further. A liturgical text is an invitation to take part in the divine office it is attached to, or at least to share in the worshipping attitude of its first users. Our understanding of the Passion narratives is bound to become deeper if, while retaining all our critical acumen, we join with the early Jerusalem Christians in their amazed contemplation of the sufferings and death of our common Lord, in their humble praise of God's saving act in Christ, in their assured hope of the resurrection of all believers. This, to my mind, is the chief contribution made by the present study.

Abbreviations

ET   English translation

JBL   *Journal of Biblical Literature*

JTS   *Journal of Theological Studies*

NTS   *New Testament Studies*

TDNT   *Theological Dictionary of the New Testament*, ET of *TWNT*, 1964–76

TWNT   *Theologisches Wörterbuch zum Neuen Testament*, ed. G. Kittel and G. Friedrich, 10 vols., 1932–79

ZNW   *Zeitschrift für die neutestamentliche Wissenschaft*

ZTK   *Zeitschrift für Theologie und Kirche*

Notes

1. Any recent biography of Jesus could offer this kind of reconstruction. Herbert Leroy, *Jesus, Überlieferung und Deutung*, Darmstadt 1978, pp. 92–128, gives a good summary of contemporary discussions about the end of Jesus' life. Among the many monographs which concentrate on the trial of Jesus, special attention should be paid to Paul Winter, *On the Trial of Jesus*, 2nd ed. revised and edited by G. Burkill and G. Vermes, Berlin 1974. An excellent little book on the last days of Jesus also deserves a mention: François Bovon, *Les derniers jours de Jésus, textes et événements*, Neuchâtel 1974.

2. The Fourth Gospel, generally considered as the latest of the canonical gospels, is usually dated about AD 100 (see e.g. the commentaries of C. K. Barrett, R. E. Brown, R. Schnackenburg and S. Schulz).

3. This remarkably early *apocryphon* can perhaps be dated about AD 150, or possibly a little earlier (see C. Maurer in E. Hennecke, *Neutestamentliche Apokryphen* I, Tübingen [3]1959, pp. 118f.; ET, *New Testament Apocrypha*, ed. R. McL. Wilson, SCM Press and Westminster Press [2]1973, vol. I, p. 180).

4. Kurt Aland has once more stated the reasons for this in his article 'Der Schluss des Markusevangeliums', published in M. Sabbe, *L'Evangile selon Marc, tradition et rédaction*, Gembloux 1974, pp. 435–70.

5. This hypothesis is just as unlikely in the slightly modified form suggested by H. W. Bartsch, who claims that the story of the empty tomb replaced that of the christophany to Peter ('Der ursprüngliche Schluss der Leidensgeschichte', in M. Sabbe, op. cit., pp. 411–33).

6. M. J. Lagrange, J. Schniewind and B. H. Streeter favoured this type of explanation of the strange ending of the Gospel of Mark.

7. Even if a book could end with *gar*, as P. W. van der Horst tried to show in his article 'Can a Book End with *gar*? A Note on Mark XVI.8', *JTS*, n.s. 23, 1972, pp. 121–4, the evasion of their duty by the women according to that verse makes an impossible conclusion.

8. I may perhaps refer to my article 'Is there a Markan Christology?' in B. Lindars and S. Smalley, eds., *Christ and Spirit in the New Testament, in honour of C. F. D. Moule*, CUP 1973, pp. 3–13.

9. See below, pp. 15–17.

10. See e.g. T. A. Burkill, *Mysterious Revelation*, Cornell University Press, Ithaca, New York 1963, pp. 218f. R. H. Lightfoot, *The Gospel Message of St Mark*, Clarendon Press 1950, pp. 48–59, put special emphasis on the features in Mark 13 which prepare the way for the Passion narrative.

11. This somewhat provocative definition of Mark 1–13 goes back to

Martin Kähler, who coined it in 1892 in his small book *Der sogennante historische Jesus und der geschichtliche, biblische Christ*, reissued Munich 1956, p. 59 n. 1; ET, *The So-called Historical Jesus and the Historic, Biblical Christ*, Fortress Press, Philadelphia, 1964, p. 80 n. 11.

12. I have tried to give a full justification of this hypothesis in my book *The Formation of the Gospel According to Mark*, SPCK 1975, Westminster Press 1976, pp. 215–59.

13. See above, n. 11.

14. R. Bultmann, *Die Geschichte der synoptischen Tradition*, Göttingen [7]1967, p. 397; ET, *The History of the Synoptic Tradition*, Blackwell, Oxford, and Harper & Row, New York, [2]1968, p. 371.

15. Since the author of the Gospel according to Luke seems to have used as his source a copy of the Markan gospel ending at 13.37.

16. K. L. Schmidt, *Der Rahmen der Geschichte Jesu, literarkritische Untersuchungen zur ältesten Jesusüberlieferung*, Berlin 1919, was the first exponent of the ideas of the new school, soon to be followed by Martin Dibelius, *Die Formgeschichte des Evangeliums*, Tübingen 1920, ET of 2nd ed., *From Tradition to Gospel*, 1934, reissued James Clarke 1971; also R. Bultmann, op. cit., 1st ed. 1921.

17. See e.g. Dibelius, op. cit., [3]1959, pp. 178–96 (ET of 2nd ed., pp. 178–96).

18. E. Linnemann, *Studien zur Passionsgeschichte*, Göttingen 1970, is a good example of the new approach, while D. Dormeyer, *Die Passion Jesu als Verhaltensmodell, literarische und theologische Analyse der Traditionsgeschichte der Markuspassion*, Münster 1974, accepts the existence of a brief narrative of the Passion as the nucleus that later redactional efforts developed, in particular by inserting isolated tradition units in that framework. The main contributions on the American side are: J. R. Donahue, *Are You the Christ? The Trial Narrative in the Gospel of Mark*, Missoula, Mont., 1973; P. J. Achtemeier, *Mark*, Fortress Press 1975; W. H. Kelber, ed., *The Passion in Mark*, Fortress Press 1976, with articles by the editor, J. R. Donahue, Norman Perrin (the teacher of most of the contributors), T. J. Weeden and others.

19. To mention only the main titles: C. H. Turner, 'Markan Usage', several articles in *JTS* 25–29, 1924–28; M. Zerwick, *Untersuchungen zum Markus-Stil*, Rome 1937; J. C. Doudna, *The Greek of the Gospel of Mark*, Studies in Biblical Literature Monograph Series V, No. 12, Philadelphia 1961; F. Neirynck, *Duality in Mark. Contributions to the Study of the Markan Redaction*, Leuven University Press 1972. The extremely cautious conclusions of Zerwick, op. cit., pp. 139–42, are typical and make no effort to define Mark's style.

20. E. J. Pryke, *Redactional Style in the Markan Gospel. A Study of Syntax and Vocabulary as Guides to Redaction in Mark*, CUP 1978, p. 31.

21. Pryke, op. cit., pp. 87–135.

22. Pryke, op. cit., pp. 32–61. As Zerwick, op. cit., p. 138, aptly puts it, parenthetical clauses simply show 'the inartistic, unreflective style of a simple narrator who does not achieve any literary mastery over a mass of material, but rather writes what he has to write just as it comes to him'.

23. Pryke, op. cit., pp. 62–7. See J. H. Moulton, *A Grammar of New Testament Greek*, vol. III, *Syntax*, by N. Turner, T. & T. Clark 1963, pp. 322f., for examples of the frequent misuse of the genitive absolute in *koinē* Greek.

24. Pryke, op. cit., pp. 67–70.

25. Pryke, op. cit., pp. 70–72. The only use of *polla* which could perhaps be described as 'extremely characteristic' (M. J. Lagrange, *Evangile selon Saint Marc*, Paris 1911, p. LXV), is its use as an adverb, not as an accusative.

26. Pryke, op. cit., pp. 73–9. Zerwick, op. cit., pp. 39–48, is particularly enlightening on that point.

27. Pryke, op. cit., pp. 79–87. Vincent Taylor, *The Gospel according to St Mark*, Macmillan ²1966, pp. 48 and 63f., gives a good summary of discussion about that phrase.

28. Mark 1.1–3.12: the gospel proclaimed to the crowds; 3.15–6.13: the Twelve called, trained and sent; 6.14–8.29: the duties of the Twelve as shepherds of the crowds; 8.22–10.52 (slightly overlapping with the previous section): all disciples must learn to suffer, like their Master; 11.1–13.37: the final victory over the bad shepherds.

29. See above, p. 11.

30. See Ernest Best, *The Temptation and the Passion: the Markan Soteriology*, CUP 1965, pp. 140–9. The contrast between Mark 10.45 and the eucharistic words of Jesus is particularly striking if the former text is understood in connection with the Jewish idea of the meaning of martyrdom as expressed in II Macc. 7.37f.; IV Macc. 6.27ff.; 17.2; 18.4, etc. (see W. H. C. Frend, *Martyrdom and Persecution in the Early Church. A Study of Conflict from the Maccabees to Donatus*, Blackwell 1966, Doubleday, New York, 1967, pp. 31–78). This suggestion, made more than twenty years ago by C. K. Barrett (in 'The Background of Mark X. 45', in *New Testament Essays: Studies in memory of T. W. Manson*, ed. A. J. B. Higgins, Manchester University Press 1959, p. 1–18), remains an attractive solution to a complex problem.

31. See below, pp. 67–82.

32. As I tried to show in *The Formation of . . . Mark*, pp. 224–48.

33. To this day the best study of the Matthaean Passion narrative remains N. A. Dahl, 'Die Passionsgeschichte bei Matthäus', in *NTS* 2, 1955–56, pp. 17–32.

34. See also P. Benoît, 'La mort de Judas', in his volume of collected articles, *Exégèse et théologie* I, Paris 1961, pp. 340–59; P. Bonnard, *L'Evangile selon saint Matthieu*, Neuchâtel 1963, pp. 393f.; A. Ogawa, *L'histoire de Jésus chez Matthieu*, Frankfurt am Main 1979, pp. 105–10.

35. A good discussion of the problems connected with the latter allusion can be found in K. Stendahl, *The School of St Matthew and its Use of the Old Testament*, 2nd ed., Lund n.d. (1968), pp. 140f.

36. Some excellent remarks on the present debate in K. Tagawa, 'People and Community in the Gospel of Matthew', *NTS* 16, 1969–70, pp. 149–62, and in Ogawa, op. cit., passim.

37. Best expressed by A. M. Farrer ('On Dispensing with Q', in *Studies in the Gospels, Essays in Memory of R. H. Lightfoot*, ed. D. E. Nineham, Blackwell 1955, pp. 55–88), the hypothesis that sees Mark and Matthew as the two

main sources of Luke served a purpose by compelling New Testament scholars to set aside the old assumptions about Q, but it cannot overcome a number of difficulties and is therefore generally rejected. See e.g. E. E. Ellis, *The Gospel of Luke*, Nelson 1966, pp. 21–30; B. Rigaux, *Témoignage de l'Evangile de Matthieu*, Bruges and Paris 1967, pp. 162–9; and his *Témoignage de l'Evangile de Luc*, Bruges and Paris 1970, pp. 71–81.

38. W. R. Farmer (e.g. his book on *The Synoptic Problem*, Macmillan 1964) and his 'Griesbachian' school may have revived a debate that was dying out, but they have found few allies. See the apt remarks of B. Rigaux, *Témoignage de Luc*, pp. 61–70.

39. As Sir John Hawkins pointed out seventy years ago in his study 'St Luke's Passion Narrative considered with reference to the Synoptic Problem', in W. Sanday, ed., *Studies in the Synoptic Problem*, Clarendon Press 1911, pp. 76–94.

40. This is achieved in Matt. 26.1–3 with the help of the usual redactional link between discourse and narrative: 'And it happened, when Jesus had finished all these sayings, . . .' so that the Passion narrative begins just like another narrative section of the gospel. In Luke, an additional summary describing Jesus' ministry in Jerusalem follows the apocalyptic discourse and leads on to the introductory verses of the Passion narrative, which simply continue the summary. In both cases, the seam is efficiently hidden.

41. See e.g. B. H. Streeter, *The Four Gospels. A Study of Origins*, Macmillan 1924, pp. 186f., 209–12, etc.

42. See the penetrating study of H. Schürmann, *Der Einsetzungsbericht Lc. 22.19–20. II. Teil einer quellenkritischen Untersuchung des lukanischen Abendmahlberichtes Lc. 22.7–38*, Münster 1955.

43. *Didache* 9–10 is often mentioned as a parallel that would also reflect an early eucharistic order, putting the cup before the bread, which I Cor. 10.16 might echo as well (see e.g. A. Loisy, *L'Evangile selon Luc*, Paris 1924, p. 512; H. Lietzmann, *Messe und Herrenmahl*, Bonn 1926, p. 234; ET, *Mass and Lord's Supper*, Brill, Leiden, 1953–79, pp. 189f.). Most scholars tend to reject that conjecture and favour the longer reading of Luke 22.15–20 (see e.g. J. Jeremias, *Die Abendmahlsworte Jesu*, Göttingen ³1960, pp. 133–53; ET, *The Eucharistic Words of Jesus*, new ed., SCM Press and Fortress Press 1966, pp. 139–59; Ellis, *The Gospel of Luke*, pp. 253–5).

44. See e.g. the summary of the Proto-Luke theory in F. C. Grant, *The Gospels*, Harper & Bros. 1957, Faber & Faber 1959, pp. 130f. According to F. Neirynck, 'La matière marcienne dans l'evangile de Luc' (in F. Neirynck, ed., *L'Evangile de Luc, problèmes littéraires et théologiques, Mémorial Lucien Cerfaux*, Gembloux 1973, pp. 157–201), p. 196, Vincent Taylor in his book *Behind the Third Gospel*, Clarendon Press 1926, p. 37, considered Luke 22.19a as reflecting 'the influence of Mark', whereas in his posthumous monograph *The Passion Narrative of Luke*, ed. O. E. Evans, CUP 1972, pp. 52 and 119, he half-heartedly gave up that idea (he still mentions the linguistic influence of Mark on Luke 22.19a on p. 124).

45. As Jeremias puts it (op. cit., p. 107, ET p. 113), it is 'an instance of the tendency towards the development of parallels which is so extraordinarily characteristic of the accounts of the institution'.

46. The Lukan tradition is of course almost identical with the Pauline tradition quoted in I Cor. 11.23–25, so that we can apply to Luke and Mark the remark made by Dibelius in his book *From Tradition to Gospel*, p. 207: 'The two texts, Paul and Mark, are not far removed from each other in content; they can both be conceived as derived from the same Aramaic original form.'

47. See e.g. the apt remarks of B. M. Metzger, *A Textual Commentary on the Greek New Testament*, United Bible Societies 1971, p. 177.

48. See above, p. 22.

49. The historical problem raised by the accounts of the meetings of the Sanhedrin on the occasion of the trial of Jesus cannot be discussed here. I simply claim that the tradition used by Luke had taken into account the widespread notion that a night session of the Sanhedrin in a capital case was against the law, and that, as a result of this rule, the haste of the Jewish authorities to deal with a prisoner arrested during the night could lead only to an early morning session. H. L. Strack and P. Billerbeck (*Kommentar zum Neuen Testament aus Talmud und Midrasch* I, Munich 1926, pp. 1020–25) make it quite clear that such a rule existed in later rabbinic Judaism, and we can be sure that it was known much earlier, even if we do not possess any proof that it was enforced under Sadducean high priests.

50. See e.g. H. Conzelmann, *Die Mitte der Zeit. Studien zur Theologie des Lukas*, Tübingen 1954, pp. 117–24; ET, *The Theology of St Luke*, Faber & Faber and Harper & Row 1960, pp. 137–44. The mere mention of the mocking by the soldiers at the foot of the cross (Luke 23.36f.) is all that is left in Luke of the theme of the man-handling of Jesus by the Romans.

51. Bultmann, *Synopt. Tradition*, [4]1958, p. 310 (ET, pp. 289f.), considers the Emmaus story to be the only christophany in the canonical gospels which can be called a legend, properly speaking. As for its connection with the Eucharist, see G. Schneider, *Das Evangelium nach Lukas*, 2 vols., Gütersloh and Würtzburg 1977, pp. 496f.: 'To sum up, we must ... say that the Emmaus story ... looks forward to the eucharistic fellowship of the church of Jesus, in which the risen Jesus himself is present.'

52. 'He copied Mark in blocks and interspersed other material in blocks also', says H. J. Cadbury of Luke (*The Making of Luke-Acts*, Macmillan [2]1958, pp. 94f.). Or again: 'In the ... passion narrative Luke is evidently not dependent on Mark alone, and since this other information dealt with the identical events ... he interwove or used alternatively the data from Mark with the parallel matter' (p. 95). Or again: 'He does not hesitate to leave Mark on one side in order to insert whole series of incidents, only to pick him up again near the point where he had dropped him' (p. 96). Strangely enough, Cadbury seems willing to make an exception for the Passion narrative, whereas the contrast between Luke and Mark is particularly striking in those chapters.

53. For attempts at reconstructing the pre-Lukan Passion narrative, see especially F. Rehkopf, *Die lukanische Sonderquelle, ihr Umfang und Sprachgebrauch*, Tübingen 1959, and Taylor, *The Passion Narrative of Luke*.

54. See e.g. R. Schnackenburg, *Das Johannesevangelium*, III, Freiburg 1975, pp. 406–17.

55. E. Schweizer, *EGO EIMI. Die religionsgeschichtliche Herkunft und theologische Bedeutung der johanneischen Bildreden, zugleich ein Beitrag zur Quellenfrage des vierten Evangeliums*, Göttingen 1939, pp. 87–109; E. Ruckstuhl, *Die literarische Einheit des Johannesevangeliums*, Fribourg 1951, pp. 180–205 and *passim*. As C. H. Dodd aptly puts it (*Historical Tradition in the Fourth Gospel*, CUP 1963, p. 426): 'We have to allow for the evangelist's rehandling of his traditional material, and on any showing this is considerable.'

56. I follow here R. Bultmann, *Das Evangelium des Johannes*, Göttingen 1941, p. 353 n. 4; ET, *The Gospel of John*, Blackwell and Westminster Press 1971, p. 464 n. 2; R. E. Brown, *The Gospel According to John (xiii–xxi)*, Doubleday, New York, and Geoffrey Chapman 1970, p. 550.

57. Schnackenburg, *Das Johannesevangelium* I, 1965, pp. 284–8, and III, pp. 341f. (ET of vol. I, *The Gospel of John* I, Crossroads, New York, and Burns & Oates 1980, pp. 297–301), and C. K. Barrett, *The Gospel according to St John*, SPCK and Macmillan, New York, 1955, pp. 146f. and 464, both half-heartedly accept that idea. R. E. Brown, *John (i–xii)*, 1966, pp. 58–63, thinks that the evangelist intended to refer both to the paschal lamb and to the Suffering Servant when he used the phrase 'Lamb of God'. Bultmann, *Johannesevangelium*, pp. 66f. and 524 n. 8, ET, pp. 96 and 677n., rightly states that in the evangelist's eyes 'Lamb of God' referred to the paschal lamb.

58. See e.g. M. Goguel, *Jésus*, Paris ²1950, pp. 187 and 352f.; ET, *The Life of Jesus*, Allen & Unwin 1933, pp. 430, 448–50.

59. Brown, *John (xiii–xxi)*, pp. 580–97.

60. See e.g. F. Rehkopf, op. cit., pp. 31–82, for a demonstration of an independent story of the arrest of Jesus as the main source of Luke 22.47–53, and A. Dauer, *Die Passionsgeschichte im Johannesevangelium*, Munich 1972, for a convincing plea in favour of the existence behind John 18.1–19.30 of a continuous narrative extending from the arrest to the death of Jesus.

61. Although they disagree on a number of points, several scholars who in recent years made important contributions to Johannine studies reach roughly the same conclusion about John having used (and freely redrafted) his own source for the trial of Jesus: Brown, op. cit., pp. 787–91, 828–36, etc.; F. Hahn, 'Der Prozess Jesu nach dem Johannesevangelium. Eine redaktionsgeschichtliche Untersuchung', in *Evangelisch-Katholischer Kommentar zum Neuen Testament, Vorarbeiten* II, Neukirchen, Zurich and Cologne 1970, pp. 23–96; Dauer, op. cit., pp. 62ff.; Schnackenburg, op. cit., III, pp. 247f., 258–64.

62. Hahn, op. cit., made this very clear, but none the less maintained that the Johannine story was based on an independent tradition, just as Dodd had done in his time (op. cit., pp. 82–120).

63. See above, p. 8. Verses 11–13 may, as Bultmann claims (*Johannesevangelium*, pp. 528f., ET, p. 682), have come from the same source, the end of which was replaced by the christophany to Mary Magdalene (vv. 14ff.), a creation of the evangelist. But the Passion narrative used by John ended with the story of the discovery of the empty tomb and included no appearances of the risen Christ.

64. See above, pp. 14–19 and 38–46.

65. See Dibelius, *Formgeschichte*, pp. 34–66 (ET of 2nd ed., pp. 37–69).

66. There can be no doubt that the original Passion narrative gave to the Last Supper several meanings which at that stage remained largely interwoven and implicit (Jeremias, *Abendmahlsworte*, pp. 196–246, ET, 204–62, analysed this complex in masterly fashion). But scholars do not seem to perceive the problem raised by the strange actions of the woman at Bethany and of the disciples eating and drinking in the upper room what, their Lord told them, was his body and his blood. According to the words of Jesus himself, these actions meant that their Lord was about to die a violent death, just as Hosea and Jeremiah sealed the fate of a rebellious Israel by the strange actions they carried out by order of Yahweh.

67. For a good description of life in Jerusalem in New Testament times, see J. Jeremias, *Jerusalem zur Zeit Jesu*, Göttingen ³1962; ET, *Jerusalem in the Time of Jesus*, SCM Press and Fortress Press 1969.

68. See e.g. C. Guignebert, *Le monde juif vers le temps de Jésus*, Paris 1935, pp. 41–82.

69. See e.g. P. Winter, *On the Trial of Jesus*, Berlin ²1974, pp. 62–90.

70. See e.g. H. Kosmala, 'Jerusalem', in *Biblisch-historisches Handwörterbuch*, ed. B. Reicke and L. Rost, II, Göttingen 1964, esp. cols. 829–36 and 845–7; M. Avi-Yonah, *The Holy Land. . . . A Historical Geography*, ET Baker Book House, Grand Rapids, 1966, pp. 190–95.

71. See e.g. Dibelius, *Formgeschichte*, pp. 178–218 (ET of 2nd ed., pp. 178–217), which remains to this day the best statement about the literary nature of the Passion narrative in relation to its historicity.

72. E. Ruckstuhl, *Die Chronologie des Letzten Mahles und des Leidens Jesu*, Einsiedeln 1963, pp. 36–55, pointed very effectively to the historical problems raised by that compression of so many events into so short a time.

73. One of the most attractive solutions offered was that of the use by Jesus of an archaic Jewish calendar also favoured by the Essenes, according to which the date of the Passover fell that year earlier by a few days than under the official temple calendar, so that some two or three days might have elapsed between the Last Supper and the death of Jesus. This hypothesis was brilliantly launched by Annie Jaubert, *La date de la Cène, calendrier biblique et liturgie chrétienne*, Paris 1957, and found a few resolute supporters, e.g. M. Black, 'The Arrest and Trial of Jesus and the Date of the Last Supper' in *New Testament Essays* (see n. 30 above), pp. 19–33, and Ruckstuhl, op. cit., pp. 55–124. But it failed to convince the majority of scholars (for the arguments against it see e.g. J. Blinzler, 'Qumran-Kalendar und Passionschronologie', *ZNW* 49, 1958, pp. 238–51), probably because it was linked with a somewhat naïve reconstruction of the events of the Passion. Historians might be well advised to have second thoughts about it.

74. J. Blinzler, *Der Prozess Jesu*, Regensburg ⁴1969, pp. 220–35, offers a spirited defence of the historicity of the Barabbas episode.

75. Mishnah Sanhedrin 4.1. The mishnaic rules of procedure may of course not have been enforced before AD 70, since the Pharisaic rabbis who later wrote the Mishnah were in the minority in the Jerusalem Sanhedrin before that date (Blinzler, *Prozess*, pp. 154–63). But many of these rules were not distinctly Pharisaic and were probably accepted by all parties among the Jews long before the destruction of the temple.

76. See below, p. 79.

77. C. Guignebert, *Jésus*, Paris [2]1969, pp. 427–510, and B. Lindars, *New Testament Apologetic. The Doctrinal Significance of the Old Testament Quotations*, SCM Press 1961, Westminster Press 1962, pp. 75–137, are among the scholars who gave a sensible version of that hypothesis, which was all too often brought into disrepute by the attempts made to use it as evidence against the historical existence of Jesus.

78. See e.g. A. Dupont-Sommer, *Les écrits esséniens découvertes près de la Mer Morte*, Paris 1959, pp. 267–70, ET, *The Essene Writings from Qumran*, Blackwell 1961, Meridian Books, New York, 1962, pp. 255–8.

79. 4Q Testimonia and 4Q Florilegium in the Qumran library are such collections. First published by J. M. Allegro in *JBL* 75, 1956, pp. 182–7, and *JBL* 77, 1958, pp. 350–54, these two texts were well analysed by Dupont-Sommer, op. cit., pp. 323–33, ET, pp. 310–19.

80. P. Prigent, *Les Testimonia dans le christianisme primitif: l'épître de Barnabé, I–XVI et ses sources*, Paris 1961 (the state of the question on the use of testimonies in early Christianity, pp. 16–28); P. Prigent, *Justin et l'Ancien Testament*, Paris 1964, pp. 9–13 and *passim*.

81. J. Héring, *La première épître de saint Paul aux Corinthiens*, Neuchâtel 1949, pp. 134f., discussed the difficulty quite openly, whereas too many scholars try to evade it, as though their authority was at stake: see e.g. the superficial assertions of H. Conzelmann, *Der erste Brief an die Korinther*, Göttingen 1969, pp. 300f. and 302, ET, *I Corinthians* (Hermeneia), Fortress Press, Philadelphia, 1975, pp. 255f.

82. C. S. C. Williams, *A Commentary on the Acts of the Apostles*, A. & C. Black [2]1964, Harper and Bros. 1958, pp. 264f.

83. See above, p. 23.

84. See e.g. C. H. Dodd, *According to the Scriptures. The Sub-structure of New Testament Theology*, Nisbet, London, 1952, Scribner's, New York, 1953, esp. ch. 3, 'The Bible of the Early Church', pp. 61–110.

85. As Dodd claimed, op. cit., pp. 88–103.

86. See e.g. H. W. Wolff, *Jesaja 53 im Urchristentum*, Berlin [3]1952, pp. 57f., and 75–9; J. Jeremias, 'Pais theou im Neuen Testament', *TWNT* 5, 1954, pp. 698–713, esp. 703–9, ET, *TDNT* 5, 1967, pp. 700–17, esp. 705–12; Lindars, *New Testament Apologetic*, pp. 45–66.

87. See e.g. Lindars, op. cit., pp. 88–110, and, in a different perspective, A. Suhl, *Die Funktion der alttestamentlichen Zitate und Anspielungen im Markus-evangelium*, Gütersloh 1965, pp. 45–66.

88. R. Morgenthaler, *Statistik des neutestamentlichen Wortschatzes*, Zurich and Frankfurt 1958, pp. 101, 112.

89. See e.g. C. H. Dodd, *The Apostolic Preaching and its Developments*, Hodder & Stoughton 1936, who applies the word only to the christological core of Christian missionary preaching; and R. Bultmann, *Theologie des Neuen Testaments*, Tübingen [7]1977, (ET of 1st ed., *Theology of the New Testament*, 2 vols., SCM Press and Scribners 1952–55), who uses it to describe the whole of the budding theology of the early church and the Hellenistic churches before and beside Paul.

90. This definition of *kerygma* is of course very similar to Dodd's.

91. Bultmann, *Synopt. Tradition*, ⁴1958, 297–308; ET, ²1968, pp. 275–84.

92. See e.g. Vincent Taylor, *Mark*, pp. 524–6 and 653–64, whose Narrative A is only a slightly expanded form of the *kerygma*, and Jeremias, *Abendmahlsworte*, pp. 83–90, ET, *Eucharistic Words*, pp. 89–96.

93. Bultmann, *Synopt. Tradition*, pp. 282–97, ET, pp. 262–74.

94. See e.g. Jeremias, op. cit., pp. 83–131, ET, pp. 89–137; Dormeyer, *Die Passion Jesu als Verhaltensmodell*, pp. 88–110; R. Pesch, *Das Markus-evangelium* II, Freiburg 1977, pp. 340–77.

95. Bultmann, *Synopt. Tradition*, pp. 297–308, ET, pp. 275–84. The other argument which he mentions on p. 298 (=276), based on the presence of so-called 'doublets' in Mark 14.17–15.1 on the one hand, and Luke 22.14–66 on the other, cannot be taken seriously. It is simply evidence for a different tradition of the Passion narrative behind Luke.

96. See e.g. Th. Boman, *Die Jesus-Überlieferung im Lichte der neueren Volkskunde*, Göttingen 1967, pp. 9–61.

97. See e.g. B. Gerhardsson, *Memory and Manuscript. Oral Tradition and Written Transmission in Rabbinic Judaism and Early Christianity*, Lund and Copenhagen 1961.

98. This hypothesis, which is accepted only by a minority of scholars, goes back to Adolf Harnack, 'Die Verklärungsgeschichte Jesu, der Bericht des Paulus und die beiden Christusvisionen des Petrus', in *Sitzungsberichte der Berliner Akademie der Wissenschaften, Phil.-hist. Klasse*, 1922, pp. 62ff.

99. E. Lohmeyer, *Das Evangelium des Markus*, Göttingen 1937, pp. 164f., was first to suggest it. He was followed by, among others, W. Grundmann (*Das Evangelium nach Markus*, Berlin 1959, pp. 169f., 225), S. E. Johnson (*A Commentary on the Gospel According to St Mark*, A. & C. Black 1960, Harper & Row 1961, pp. 148–50), and E. Haenchen (*Der Weg Jesu. Eine Erklärung des Markus-Evangeliums und der kanonischen Parallelen*, Berlin 1966, pp. 295f.).

100. See above, pp. 24, 35, 45.

101. To take but a few significant examples (see Streeter, *The Four Gospels*, pp. 186–91, and T. W. Manson, *The Sayings of Jesus*, 1949, reissued SCM Press and Eerdmans 1971, pp. 11–21, 105f., 108–10, 122–4, 131f., 135–45, 179–82), the same tradition in three different forms that existed before the gospels is still visible behind Mark 1.1–8 and parallels, Mark 1.9–13 and parr., Mark 3.22–30 and parr., Mark 4.21–25, 30–32 and parr., Mark 6.8–10 and parr., Mark 8.34f., 38 and parr., Mark 9.50 and parr., and Mark 10.11f. and parr.

102. See e.g. W. G. Kümmel, *Einleitung in das Neue Testament*, Heidelberg ¹⁸1976, p. 37, ET of 17th ed., *Introduction to the New Testament*, Abingdon Press and SCM Press 1975, p. 46.

103. Jeremias, *Abendmahlsworte*, pp. 132–95, ET, *Eucharistic Words*, pp. 138–203.

104. With all due respect to Jeremias, it must be said that his short demonstration of the independence of the story of the Last Supper (op. cit pp. 95–99, ET, pp. 101–5), based on Paul's quotation of it in I Cor. 11. 23–25, only suggests that the apostle knew the Passion narrative as part of the Jerusalem tradition.

105. J. Munck, 'Discours d'adieu dans le Nouveau Testament et dans la

littérature biblique', in *Aux sources de la tradition chrétienne. Mélanges offerts à M. Maurice Goguel*, Neuchâtel and Paris 1950, pp. 155–70; H. Schürmann, *Jesu Abschiedsrede, Lk 22.21–38*, Münster 1957, esp. pp. 63–139; G. Schneider, *Das Evangelium nach Lukas*, Gütersloh and Würzburg 1977, pp. 449–56.

106. Pesch, *Das Markusevangelium* II, p. 319, no doubt goes a little too far when he writes: 'From Mark 14.1 Mark follows the pre-Markan Passion narrative ... The evangelist has not inserted anything into the tradition that had come down to him ...'; but he is not far out.

107. I claim responsibility for this hypothesis (see my *Formation of ... Mark*, pp. 236–8), but it is a very common conjecture that Mark 14.28, which is missing in the Fayyum fragment, was not part of the Passion narrative in its pre-Markan form, but was added to it editorially; E. Lohmeyer, op. cit., pp. 311f., was followed by, among others, Grundmann, Johnson and Haenchen, opp. citt., ad loc., as well as by W. Marxsen, *Der Evangelist Markus*, Göttingen ²1959, pp. 47–59, ET, *Mark the Evangelist, Studies on the Redaction History of the Gospel*, Abingdon Press 1969, pp. 75–92.

108. See above, p. 59.

109. See e.g. Barrett, *John*, pp. 436f.; Brown, *John (xiii–xxi)*, pp. 834–6; Schnackenburg, *Das Johannesevangelium* III, pp. 263f.

110. See above, p. 21.

111. See e.g. Schneider, *Lukas*, p. 484; Schnackenburg, op. cit., pp. 306f.

112. See above, p. 39.

113. See above, p. 39.

114. See above, pp. 28f.

115. See above, p. 40.

116. Jeremias, *Abendmahlsworte*, pp. 73–7, ET, *Eucharistic Words*, pp. 79–84.

117. Bultmann, *Das Evangelium des Johannes*, 1941, pp. 161f., 360, 370f., ET, *John*, pp. 218–20, 472, 485f. Schnackenburg, op. cit., pp. 48–53, considers the Fourth Gospel as 'sakramentskritisch', not as 'antisakramental', but finds the omission of the story of the institution of the Eucharist incompatible with any sacramental interpretation of the Fourth Gospel.

118. By omitting any mention of a mocking by the crowd, as well as by recording the repentance of the people (Luke 23.48), Luke prepares the scene for the success of the apostles' preaching to the multitudes in Jerusalem (Acts 2.36–41 etc.). A. Loisy, *L'Evangile selon Luc*, Paris 1924, pp. 557f., is aware of the editorial activity of the evangelist, but makes no attempt to account for it.

119. The hypothesis of R. Pesch (*Das Markusevangelium* I, Freiburg 1976, p. 67, II, 1977, pp. 1–27), who includes Mark 8.27–33; 9.2–13, 30–35; 10.1, 32–34, 46–52; 11.1–23, 27–33; 12.1–12, 13–17, 34c, 35–37, 41–44; 13.1f., as well as 14.1–16.8, in the pre-Markan Passion narrative is an interesting attempt to leave the beaten track. Unfortunately it is based on arguments about style, use of scripture and literary structure which I find totally unconvincing as far as chs. 8–13 are concerned.

120. See e.g. Tobit 14.3–11; I Macc. 2.49–68; II Macc. 7.20–23, 27–29, 30–38; IV Macc. 16.15–23; 18.6–19; IV Ezra 14.27–36; II Baruch 77–86;

I Enoch 91ff.; Assumption of Moses 1–10; Jubilees 20–22; Testaments of the Twelve Patriarchs, etc. See the valuable comments on those texts by Munck, 'Discours d'adieu . . .', *Mélanges . . . Goguel*, pp. 156– 9.

121. The phrases *to pascha thuein* (Mark 14.12 and parr.), *to pascha esthiein* (Mark 14.12, 14 and parr.) and *to paschahetoimazein* (Mark 14.16 and parr.) leave no doubt about it, owing to their use in the Septuagint (J. Jeremias, '*Pascha*' in *TWNT* V, p. 896 n. 8, ET, *TDNT* V, p. 897 n. 8).

122. See above, pp. 52f.

123. See above, p. 59.

124. The custom of praying three times a day became established among Jews only during the last two centuries BC (see Ps. 55.17 and Dan. 6.11–14) and, after some changes connected, it seems, with the growth of synagogues and the destruction of the temple, took its final form in the Mishnah (Berakoth 2.3; 5.4; 6.2). The three hours of prayer were always, as far as we know, attached to the beginning or the end of the three-hour periods between 6 a.m. and 6 p.m. See e.g. E. Schürer, *Geschichte des jüdischen Volkes im Zeitalter Jesu Christi* §24.iv, Vol. II, Leipzig ³1898, pp. 186ff., ET, *A History of the Jewish People in the Time of Christ*, rev. ed, II, T. & T. Clark, Edinburgh, 1979, p. 303 n. 40.

125. See e.g. J. Carmignac, *Recherches sur le 'Notre Père'*, Paris 1969.

126. Bultmann, *Synopt. Tradition*, sees no hymn or confession of faith in the synoptic tradition, while Oscar Cullmann (*La foi et la culte de l'Eglise primitive*, Neuchâtel 1963, pp. 49–87) studies the earliest Christian creeds without referring to the gospels, apart from a few minor allusions.

127. J. Potin, *La fête juive de la Pentecôte*, 2 vols., Paris 1971.

128. On the relationship between the book of Esther and the feast of Purim, see e.g. A. Lods, *Histoire de la littérature hébraïque et juive depuis les origines jusqu'à la ruine de l'Etat juif (135 après J.C.)*, Paris 1950, pp. 793–807.

129. On the evolution of the Passover celebration, see e.g. T. H. Gaster, *Passover. Its History and Traditions*, Abelard-Schuman, New York, 1958. On the Passover Haggadah, see E. D. Goldschmidt, *The Passover Haggadah. Its Sources and History* (in Hebrew), Jerusalem 1960.

130. Philip Carrington, *The Primitive Christian Calendar. A Study in the Making of the Marcan Gospel* I, CUP 1952.

131. See e.g. W. Rordorf, *Der Sonntag, Geschichte des Ruhe- und Gottesdiensttages im ältesten Christentum*, Zurich 1962, ET, *Sunday, the History of the Day of Rest and Worship in the Earliest Centuries of the Christian Church*, SCM Press and Westminster Press 1968; also S. Bacchiocchi, *From Sabbath to Sunday, a Historical Investigation of the Rise of Sunday Observance in Early Christianity* Rome 1977.

132. See e.g. M. Goguel, *L'Eglise primitive*, Paris 1947, pp. 411–16, ET, *The Primitive Church*, Allen & Unwin and Macmillan, New York, 1964, pp. 386–91.

133. Apart from the books of Gaster and Goldschmidt mentioned in n. 129 above, see also D. Daube, *The New Testament and Rabbinic Judaism*, Athlone Press, London, 1956, pp. 163–9 and 186–95, and R. Le Déaut, *La nuit pascale, essai sur la signification de la Pâque juive à partir du Targum d'Exode XII 42*, Rome 1963.

134. Jeremias, *Abendmahlsworte*, pp. 36–8, ET, pp. 42–4.

135. J. Leipoldt, *Der Gottesdienst der ältesten Kirche*, Leipzig 1937, p. 21, and F. F. Bruce, *Commentary on the Book of Acts*, Marshall, Morgan & Scott, London, ²1965, pp. 82f., are a little isolated when they suggest that early Jerusalem Christians attended sacrificial worship services in the temple. Goguel, op. cit., pp. 272f., ET, pp. 262f., holds the majority view that they did not, but is not typical in his attempt to justify this view; most scholars simply consider this self-evident. As a matter of fact, we have no clear evidence one way or the other. But the temple was doubtless a sacred place where they endeavoured to go and pray frequently, as the traditional story of the cleansing of the temple shows (see E. Trocmé, 'L'expulsion des marchands du temple', *NTS* 15, 1968–69, pp. 1–22).

136. It is not possible simply to brush aside Acts 20.16b, which states that Paul was doing all he could in order to be in Jerusalem on the day of Pentecost, since this verse comes from the travel diary and plays no part in the editorial sections of the narrative in ch. 21, as would no doubt have been the case if Luke had invented Paul's wish (see E. Trocmé, *Le 'Livre des Actes' et l'histoire*, Paris 1957, pp. 128–49). If so, Paul could only have one reason for hastening to get to Jerusalem in time for one of the main festivals of the Jewish year: to take part in the pilgrimage to the temple. The scholars who try to do away with that feature of Paul's tempestuous biography simply forget that even the fiercest rebels sometimes have no other choice than to 'go to Canossa'. Even though Paul himself (see Rom. 15.14–29) and Luke (who drastically plays down the themes of the collection, Acts 24.17, and of the pilgrimage, Acts 20.16b) do their best to hide that fact, Paul's last journey to Jerusalem was little short of an act of submission to the law of Moses.

137. G. Schille, 'Das Leiden des Herrn. Die evangelische Passionstradition und ihr "Sitz im Leben"', *ZTK* 52, 1955, pp. 161–205.

138. Acts 1–2 suggests that the disciples stayed in Jerusalem after their Master's death and that they preached the gospel in public no more than seven weeks after the Resurrection. Most scholars agree that a scattering of the disciples in Palestine after the crucifixion took place before a group of them settled in Jerusalem again. There is no agreement as to the date of that settlement, apart from a general recognition that it could not be placed more than two or three years after the crucifixion, since Paul found a well-established church at the time of his first visit to Jerusalem before the end of the thirties (see e.g. J. Finegan, *Handbook of Biblical Chronology*, Princeton University Press 1964, pp. 285–325).

139. Along the lines suggested by the vigorous claim to historical reliability made by, e.g., Jaubert, *La date de la Cène*, pp. 105–36, on behalf of the whole of the four Passion narratives, or by A. Feuillet, *L'agonie de Gethsemani, enquête exégétique et théologique*, Paris 1977, pp. 42–53 and 232–8, as regards the scene of the agony in the garden.

140. The scanty bits of information we possess on the fate of the Jerusalem church in that difficult time (mostly derived from the *Ecclesiastical History* of Eusebius) are put to good use in, e.g., J. Lebreton and J. Zeiller, *L'Eglise primitive*, Paris 1946, pp. 242–4 and 393f.

141. See above, pp. 78–80.
142. See e.g. Finegan, op. cit., pp. 33–57; Jaubert, op. cit., pp. 11–75 and 105–59; Ruckstuhl, *Die Chronologie des Letzten Mahles*, pp. 67–124.
143. See above, pp. 53f.
144. See above, pp. 51f.
145. See e.g. Dibelius, *Formgeschichte*, pp. 184–9 (ET of 2nd ed., pp. 183–9); C. Maurer, 'Knecht Gottes und Sohn Gottes im Passionsbericht des Markusevangeliums', *ZTK* 50, 1953, pp. 1–38; Lindars, *New Testament Apologetic*, pp. 75–137 and 251–9; Suhl, *Die Funktion der alttestamentlichen Zitate*, pp. 26–66.
146. See e.g. O. Cullman, *Die Christologie des Neuen Testaments*, Tübingen 1957, ET, *The Christology of the New Testament*, SCM Press and Westminster Press ²1963; F. Hahn, *Christologische Hoheitstitel. Ihre Geschichte im frühen Christentum*, Göttingen 1963, ET, *The Titles of Jesus in Christology: their History in Early Christianity*, Lutterworth Press 1969.
147. The only chritsological titles which might be considered as creations of the Hellenistic church, *Kyrios* and *Logos*, both have Jewish and Semitic roots, even if they acquired new meanings in a Greek-speaking environment outside Palestine. It is therefore likely that they were first used in the early Jerusalem church, just like all the others. As Cullmann (op. cit., p. 332, ET, p. 322) says: 'The principal themes of the New Testament Christology were already known and developed by the earliest Church.'

Index of Authors

Achtemeier, P. J., 14, 96 n. 18
Aland, K., 95 n. 4
Allegro, J. M., 102 n. 79
Avi-Yonah, M., 101 n. 70

Bacchiocchi, S., 105 n. 131
Barrett, C. K., 95 n. 2, 97 n. 30, 100 n. 57, 104 n. 109
Bartsch, H. W., 95 n. 5
Benoît, P., 97 n. 34
Best, E., 97 n. 30
Billerbeck, P., 99 n. 49
Black, M., 101 n. 73
Blinzler, J., 101 nn. 73–5
Boman, T., 103 n. 96
Bonnard, P., 97 n. 34
Bovon, F., 95 n. 1
Brown, R. E., 95 n. 2, 100 nn. 56, 57, 59, 104 n. 109
Bruce, F. F., 106 n. 135
Bultmann, R., 12, 61–3, 96 n. 14, 99 n. 51, 100 nn. 56, 57, 63, 102 n. 89, 103 nn. 91, 95, 104 n. 117, 105 n. 126
Burkill, T. A., 95 n. 10

Cadbury, H. J., 36, 99 n. 52
Carmignac, J., 105 n. 125
Carrington, P., 81f., 105 n. 130
Claudel, P., 1
Clement of Alexandria, 7
Conzelmann, H., 99 n. 50, 102 n. 81
Crashaw, R., 1
Cullmann, O., 105 n. 126, 107 nn. 146, 147

Dahl, N. A., 97 n. 33

Daube, D., 105 n. 133
Dauer, A., 100 nn. 60, 61
Dibelius, M., 50, 96 n. 16, 99 n. 46, 100 n. 65, 101 n. 71, 107 n. 145
Dodd, C. H., 100 nn. 55, 62, 102 nn. 84, 85, 89, 90
Donahue, J. R., 14, 96 n. 18
Dormeyer, D., 14, 96 n. 18, 103 n. 94
Doudna, J. C., 96 n. 19
Dupont-Sommer, A., 102 nn. 78, 79

Eliot, T. S., 1
Ellis, E. E., 98 nn. 37, 43
Ephraem Syrus, 1
Eusebius, 7, 106 n. 140

Farmer, W. R., 98 n. 38
Farrer, A. M., 97 n. 37
Feuillet, A., 106 n. 139
Finegan, J., 106 n. 138, 107 n. 142
Frend, W. H. C., 97 n. 30

Gaster, T. H., 105 nn. 129, 133
Gerhardsson, B., 103 n. 97
Goguel, M., 100 n. 58, 105 n. 132, 106 n. 135
Goldschmidt, E. D., 105 nn. 129, 133
Grant, F. C., 98 n. 44
Grundmann, W., 103 n. 99, 104 n. 107
Guignebert, C., 101 n. 68, 102 n. 72

Haenchen, E., 103 n. 99, 104 n. 107
Hahn, F., 100 nn. 61, 62, 107 n. 146

Index of Biblical References

Apocrypha and Pseudepigrapha